BTEC Level 2 First Study Skills Guide in Creative Media Production

Welcome to your Study Skills Guide! You can make it your own – start by adding your personal and course details below...

Learner's name:

BTEC course title:

Date started:

Mandatory units:

Optional units:

Centre name:

Centre address:

Tutor's name:

Hammersmith and West London College

311951

Published by Pearson Education Limited, a company incorporated in England and Wales,
having its registered office at Edinburgh Gate, Harlow, Essex, CM20 2JE. Registered company
number: 872828

Edexcel is a registered trademark of Edexcel Limited

Text © Pearson Education Limited 2010

First published 2010

13 12 11 10
10 9 8 7 6 5 4 3 2 1

British Library Cataloguing in Publication Data
A catalogue record for this book is available from the British Library

ISBN 978 1 84690 572 8

Typeset and edited by DSM Partnership
Cover design by Visual Philosophy, created by eMC Design
Cover photo © Image Source Ltd
Printed in Malaysia, KHL-CTP

Acknowledgements
The author and publisher would like to thank the following individuals and organisations for
permission to reproduce photographs:
Alamy Images: Ace Stock Limited 59, Kirsty Pargeter 80, Jacky Chapman, Janine Wiedel
Photolibrary 15; Corbis: 64, Comstock 5; iStockphoto: Alexey Ivanov 82, Dejan Ljamic 37, Andrey
Tsidvintsev 40; Pearson Education Ltd: Steve Shott 24, Ian Wedgewood 34; Pearson Education Ltd:
Photodisc. Photolink. Jack Star 79; Shutterstock: 78; TopFoto: John Powell 20.

All other images © Pearson Education

Every effort has been made to contact copyright holders of material reproduced in this book. Any
omissions will be rectified in subsequent printings if notice is given to the publishers.

Websites
Go to www.pearsonhotlinks.co.uk to gain access to the relevant website links and information on
how they can aid your studies. When you access the site, search for either the express code 5728S,
title BTEC Level 2 First Study Skills Guide in Creative Media Production or ISBN 9781846905728.

Disclaimer
This material has been published on behalf of Edexcel and offers high-quality support for the
delivery of Edexcel qualifications.
This does not mean that the material is essential to achieve any Edexcel qualification, nor does it
mean that it is the only suitable material available to support any Edexcel qualification. Edexcel
material will not be used verbatim in setting any Edexcel examination or assessment. Any resource
lists produced by Edexcel shall include this and other appropriate resources.Copies of official
specifications for all Edexcel qualifications may be found on the Edexcel website: www.edexcel.com

Contents

Popular progression pathways

General qualification	Vocationally related qualification	Applied qualification
Undergraduate Degree	BTEC Higher National	Foundation Degree
GCE AS and A level	BTEC National	Advanced Diploma
GCSE	BTEC First	Higher (L2) and Foundation (L1) Diplomas

Your BTEC First course
Early days

Every year many new learners start BTEC Level 2 First courses, enjoy the challenge and successfully achieve their award. Some do this the easy way; others make it harder for themselves.

Everyone will have different feelings when they start their course.

Three ways to make life easier

✔ **Positive thinking** This means believing that you will succeed. Your ability to do well is affected by what goes on in your mind, which influences your whole attitude.

✔ **Knowing about the course and what you have to do**. This means you focus your time and energy on what really matters.

✔ **Using this Study Skills Guide to help you!** It gives you all the information you need and will help you develop the positive thinking skills you need.

Case study: Thinking positively

Jack is preparing to begin his BTEC First in Creative Media Production. He has applied for a place on the course because it seems really exciting and interesting. He is excited by the unit on 2D computer games as the projects seem really interesting. Jack loves to play computer games and would like to work in the industry.

When he first applied, Jack just couldn't wait to get going. Now the course is about to begin he is feeling a bit nervous. Jack admits that 'I suppose that it is natural to feel a bit uneasy. This is a big step for me. I will be joining a new course, meeting new people and doing different things. I have been starting to worry about meeting new people, about whether I'll cope with the course or whether it's even the right course for me.'

Jack's tutor at school says that whenever you are feeling anxious or unsure you should think positively. So, Jack has been trying to turn his negative thoughts into positives. Here are some examples.

- Negative thought: 'I might not like or get on with the other students on the course.'

- Positive thought: 'This is a good opportunity to meet others and to improve my people skills. A job in the media involves in working with lots of different people, and this course will help prepare me for that.'

- Negative thought: 'I bet everyone will be more clever and talented than me.'

- Positive thought: 'A course on creative media production requires learners to develop a wide mix of skills, and this is a great opportunity to learn from others as well as the tutors. There might be some students who are better at drawing than me and others who know how to use a video camera, but I know a lot about computer games and I've made some pretty good Flash animations in my spare time. The other students will be in the same boat as me, and I know that if I have any problems all I need to do is ask for help.'

- Negative thought: 'I know I'm going to enjoy the units on computer games and animation but what if I really don't like some of the other units on the course?'

- Positive thought: 'The whole point of doing a course like this is to learn new skills. If I get good at a variety of things, I'm going to be in a better position when it comes to getting a job in the media sector. I'm never going to know if I like making videos until I try it, and while I might think I want to work in the games industry now, doing this course might change my mind. I might decide that I'd really rather work in advertising.'

About your course

What do you know already?

If someone asks you about your course, could you give a short, accurate description? If you can, you have a good understanding of what your course is about. This has several benefits.

Four benefits of understanding your course

1. You will be better prepared and organised.

2. You can make links between the course and the world around you.

3. You can check how your personal interests and hobbies relate to the course.

4. You will be alert to information that relates to topics you are studying, whether it's from conversations with family and friends, watching television or at a part-time job.

Read any information you have been given by your centre. Also check the Edexcel website for further details – go to www.edexcel.com.

TOP TIPS

If you have a part-time job, you're likely to be involved in helping customers and colleagues. These are important skills for any BTEC First learner.

TRY THIS

Write down your interests and hobbies and identify those that relate to your studies in any way.

Interest/hobby	How this relates to my studies

What else do you need to know?

Five facts you should find out about your course

1 The type of BTEC qualification you are studying.

2 How many credits your qualification is worth.

3 The number of mandatory units you will study and what they cover.

4 How many credits the mandatory units are worth.

5 The number of optional units you need to study in total and the options available in your centre.

BTEC FACT

BTEC First Certificate = 15 credits

BTEC First Extended Certificate = 30 credits

BTEC First Diploma = 60 credits

Generally, the more credits there are, the longer it takes to study for the qualification.

TRY THIS

Find out which optional units your centre offers. To check the topics covered in each unit go to www.pearsonhotlinks.co.uk, insert the express code 5728S and click on the link for this page.

TOP TIPS

If you have a choice of optional units in your centre and are struggling to decide, talk through your ideas with your tutor.

Case study: Course options

Sarah and Rashid are both studying for BTEC Level 2 First qualifications in Creative Media Production. Sarah is taking a BTEC First Extended Certificate at school. Her friend Rashid has joined a BTEC First Diploma course at his local further education college.

Rashid is 16. He finished his GCSEs last year, and although he got good grades in a few subjects he was disappointed in some of his results. He has decided to take a one-year course that will allow him to progress to a BTEC Level 3 Diploma next year.

Sarah is 14 and she will be taking her course over the next two years alongside several GCSEs. She feels she may be interested in working in the television industry and, like Rashid, she is considering doing a BTEC Level 3 Diploma in Media. Sarah also enjoys French and Spanish, and at the moment she can't decide between languages and her interest in media, so she is keeping her options open.

After the first day on their new courses Sarah and Rashid are chatting on the internet. They discover that there are some differences between the courses they are taking.

Rashid's course has more credits than the one Sarah is taking. Rashid is studying for his qualification in one year, while Sarah's course lasts two years. This means that Rashid has more hours timetabled for his course each week than Sarah. Other than his BTEC, the only other course Rashid is taking is a GCSE English resit.

Sarah is interested in television and film. Her course includes a specialist unit on video production. Rashid can choose two of his specialist units from a list of options. He could have picked video production but he is more interested in a career in web design, so has chosen the specialist units on web design and interactive media production. Sarah and Rashid's courses do include some similiar elements. They will both be taking a unit on the creative media sector, which will allow them to explore different career opportunities in the media.

Activity: How well do you know your course?

Complete this activity to check that you know the main facts. Compare your answers with a friend. You should have similar answers except where you make personal choices, such as about optional units. Your tutor can help you complete task 9.

1 The correct title of the BTEC award I am studying is:

2 The length of time it will take me to complete my award is:

3 The number of mandatory units I have to study is:

4 The titles of my mandatory units, and their credit values, are:

5 The main topics I will learn in each mandatory unit include:

Mandatory unit	Main topics

6 The number of credits I need to achieve by studying optional units is:

7 The titles of my optional units, and their credit values, are:

8 The main topics I will learn in each optional unit include:

Optional unit	Main topics

9 Other important aspects of my course are:

10 After I have achieved my BTEC First, my options include:

Introduction to the media sector

Choosing to study a BTEC Level 2 First in Creative Media Production is an excellent decision to make for many reasons. The media industries employ a huge number of people who undertake a wide range of job roles using an array of different skills and techniques.

When you think of the media sector, you may think of just a small part of the media, such as working in television, but the sector encompasses many different industries.

The table below lists a few examples of the different industries within the media sector. There is space at in the bottom rows of the table to add any more media industries that you can think of.

Within each media industry there is a wide range of different jobs. Choose an industry or part of the media that appeals to you, and write down as many jobs within that industry as you can think of in the appropiate space in the second column.

Industry	Job roles
Television and film	
Newspapers and magazines	
Web design	
Games design	

Other media industries that you may have added to the table include animation, advertising and photography.

You might have listed some of these roles:
- within television and film there are camera operators, scriptwriters, directors, video editors, sound mixers, graphic designers, researchers, storyboard artists, visual effects teams and many more
- jobs within newspapers and magazines include journalist, editor, graphic designer and photographer
- careers in web design could involve working on the visual design of websites, creating animations for websites, writing the programming code or databases for them, or even presenting and selling ideas for websites to clients
- within the games design sector there are games testers, concept artists, 3D modellers and programmers.

Many media jobs will involve you working as part of a large team, but in some cases you may work alone, or in a small team, and have to be able to take on several roles.

Which of the jobs you have listed appeal to you?

The media industries

In order to cover the skills and techniques for the many possible career paths in the media sector, the BTEC Level 2 First in Creative Media Production has a wide variety of units. Some schools and colleges may give you a choice of units, while others may make the selection that they feel is best for learners. These units will help you decide which of the industries within the media sector you might like to specialise in.

If you decide to progress to BTEC Level 3 National in Creative Media Production you may have a choice of specialist pathways. The units you experience on your BTEC Level 2 First will help you choose which pathway you want to study later. Your choice of pathways on the BTEC Level 3 National might include:
- television and film
- radio
- sound recording
- print-based media
- interactive media
- games development.

Case study: Alishea's route into radio

Alishea completed her BTEC Level 2 First in Media in 2002 and has since gone on to work as broadcast technician at a commercial local radio station.

'When I decided to do a BTEC Level 2 First in Media at school, at the time I thought I might like to work in the television industry, but I wasn't really sure. I have always liked music and found that I really enjoyed the audio production unit on the course. I was very good at it too, and got a distinction for this unit. So I decided to go to college to do a BTEC Level 3 National in Media, specialising in the radio pathway. This led to me taking a foundation degree in sound engineering, which I finally completed in 2009.

'Near the end of my foundation degree course I had some work experience with a local hospital radio station, and this gave me the skills and confidence to apply for a position as a broadcast technician at the local commercial radio station. The interview went well, but I was still very surprised and over the moon when I found out that I'd got the job.

'Working on live broadcasts is great fun, but very hard work. It's quite scary to think of how many people are listening if I make any mistakes. We work as a close team with the producers and presenters and rely a lot on each other. The training I did both at school and in college has really provided me with a good starting point for my career.'

Skills you need for your sector

You will develop a range of specialist skills in completing your BTEC Level 2 First in Creative Media Production. For example, you may learn to operate the various specialist software programs that are widely used in the media. Many jobs in the media sector rely on information technology, and so many units will develop your IT skills in areas such as web authoring, interactive media production and digital graphics. You will also learn how to communicate your ideas visually by means of sketches and storyboards.

It is important to realise that not everybody will be good at everything. Some people may pick up computer skills more quickly than others, but feel less confident about drawing their ideas on paper. However, it is important you put in the effort to develop all your skills, especially in any areas in which you feel that you may be weaker.

Many personal, learning and thinking skills (PLTS) are essential in the media. For example, you will need to show teamworking and creative thinking skills in presentations and discussions. All learners will develop these skills regardless of the specialist units they are taking. The skills listed below will be even more important for your future career development.

○ **How to develop ideas**
When working on a new project within the media sector, whether it is a script or storyboard for a film or radio show, or visuals for a website or game character, you will need to be able to come up with a variety of ideas, develop them and be able to communicate them to others.

- **How to work as part of a team**
  Teamwork is crucial within many industries of the media sector. The team for a television drama will include directors, scriptwriters, camera operators and lighting engineers; radio presenters rely on researchers, producers, sound engineers; web designers need programmers to make the sites work technically etc.

- **How to research information properly**
  Research skills are important, whether you are researching the content for a website, video or magazine, or you are developing ideas for a new game or magazine and you are trying to find out what the target audience would be interested in.

- **How to plan a project properly and make sure you meet deadlines**
  Deadlines are crucial in the media sector, whether for the launch of a magazine, game or film, or the broadcast of a television programme, radio show or advert. Proper planning is essential, not only to make sure that deadlines are met, but to ensure that the work is of good quality and meets the needs of the client.

- **Communication and presentation skills**
  Both written and spoken communication skills are important within media industries. Many jobs within the media sector will require you to write content for products such as websites and film and animation scripts, or will require you to present proposals to clients or to other people within your organisation.

In the mandatory units you will learn about the creative media industries, about how media products are designed to meet audience needs, and about the kinds of skills needed to help you obtain employment in a creative media industry.

Regardless of the pathway you are studying, there are some essential personal, learning and thinking skills that you will develop while you are completing your BTEC programme. See page 93 for more information.

Your BTEC course will help you develop all-round skills, like communication.

More about BTEC Level 2 Firsts

What is different about a BTEC Level 2 First?

How you learn

Expect to be 'hands-on'. BTEC Level 2 Firsts are practical and focus on the skills and knowledge needed in the workplace. You will learn new things and learn how to apply your knowledge.

BTEC First learners are expected to take responsibility for their own learning and be keen and well-organised. You should enjoy having more freedom, while knowing you can still ask for help or support if you need it.

How you are assessed

Many BTEC First courses are completed in one year, but if you are taking GCSEs as well, you may be doing it over two years or more. You will be assessed by completing **assignments** written by your tutors. These are based on **learning outcomes** set by Edexcel. Each assignment will have a deadline.

Case study: The first assignments

Daniel looks back at the assignments he completed in his first term on the BTEC Level 2 First in Creative Media Production

'Our first assignment was for Unit 3: The Creative Media Sector. We had to research a job in the media, and I chose a camera operator.

'I spent time in the college library and also searched for articles on the internet. I was very lucky that we went on a visit to a TV studio where I interviewed a camera operator to find out more about the job.

'We presented our findings to the rest of the class using PowerPoint slides. I was quite nervous, but the presentation went well and I was awarded the merit grading criteria relating to this assignment.

'The second assignment covered parts of the advertising production and video production units. We had to work as a group to develop ideas for a television advert for a local car dealership. We met with the manager of the car dealership to find out what sort of advert he wanted. Then we met as a group to discuss our ideas. Next we had to decide who would take which role in the filming, which we will do next term.

'In the first assignment I was managing my own time and work. In the second assignment I am working much more closely with the members of my group to discuss and develop ideas. I feel that I really have to try to do well, not just for myself but also for the sake of the others. I'm really looking forward to filming the adverts and showing them to the manager of the car dealership. I think that if he likes our advert, it will make all the hard work worthwhile.'

Getting the most from your BTEC

Getting the most from your BTEC involves several skills, such as using your time effectively and working well with other people. Knowing yourself is also important.

Knowing yourself

How would you describe yourself? Make some notes here.

If you described yourself to someone else, would you be able to sum up your temperament and personality, identify your strengths and weaknesses and list your skills? If not, is it because you've never thought about it or because you honestly don't have a clue?

Learning about yourself is often called self-analysis. You may have already done personality tests or careers profiles. If not, there are many available online. However, the information you gain from these profiles is useless unless you can apply it to what you are doing.

Your personality

Everyone is different. For example, some people:

- like to plan in advance; others prefer to be spontaneous
- love being part of a group; others prefer one or two close friends
- enjoy being the life and soul of the party; others prefer to sit quietly and feel uncomfortable at large social gatherings
- are imaginative and creative; others prefer to deal only with facts
- think carefully about all their options before making a decision; others follow their 'gut instincts' and often let their heart rule their head.

Case study: Personality types – Marcus and Emma

Many people think that certain personality types will do better on a BTEC First programme than others, but this isn't necessarily the case.

Take Emma and Marcus. Both are taking a BTEC Level 2 First in Creative Media Production, but they have very different personalities.

Emma has a bubbly and outgoing personality. She is always full of ideas and loves to present them to the rest of the class. Sometimes however she is a bit bossy – she tends to think her ideas are the best so won't listen to contributions from other people. She can also be a bit disorganised and finds it hard to settle down to work for long periods of time without getting distracted, so Emma sometimes finds it hard to meet deadlines.

Marcus, on the other hand, is well organised and conscientious. He sets himself high standards and will spend a long time working at home trying to get his projects finished in the way that he wants them. However, he would rather just work on the first idea he has rather than discuss and develop a number of ideas. He is reluctant to share his ideas with others. He doesn't like working as part of a group, so he sometimes takes a back seat when decisions are being made.

Do you recognise any of your own personality traits in Emma and Marcus?

In what ways do you think that your personality is suited to the creative media production course?

TRY THIS

Imagine one of your friends is describing your best features. What would they say?

Personalities in the workplace

There's a mix of personalities in most workplaces. Some people prefer to work behind the scenes, such as many IT practitioners, who like to concentrate on tasks they enjoy doing. Others love high-profile jobs where they may often be involved in high-pressure situations, such as paramedics and television presenters. Most people fall somewhere between these two extremes.

In any job there will be some aspects that are more appealing and interesting than others. If you have a part-time job you will already know this. The same thing applies to any course you take!

Your personality and your BTEC First course

Understanding your personality means you can identify which parts of your course you are likely to find easy and which more difficult. Working out the aspects you need to develop should be positive. You can also think about how your strengths and weaknesses may affect other people.

- Natural planners find it easier to schedule work for assignments.
- Extroverts like giving presentations and working with others but may overwhelm quieter team members.
- Introverts often prefer to work alone and may be excellent at researching information.

> ## BTEC FACT
>
> All BTEC First courses enable you to develop your personal, learning and thinking skills (**PLTS**), which will help you to meet new challenges more easily. (See page 93.)

Activity: What is your personality type?

1a) Identify your own personality type, either by referring to a personality test you have done recently or by going online and doing a reliable test. Go to www.pearsonhotlinks.co.uk, insert the express code 5728S and click on the link for this activity.

Print a summary of the completed test or write a brief description of the results for future reference.

b) Use this information to identify the tasks and personal characteristics that you find easy or difficult.

	Easy	Difficult
Being punctual		
Planning how to do a job		
Working neatly and accurately		
Being well organised		
Having good ideas		
Taking on new challenges		
Being observant		
Working with details		
Being patient		
Coping with criticism		
Dealing with customers		
Making decisions		
Keeping calm under stress		
Using your own initiative		

	Easy	Difficult
Researching facts carefully and accurately		
Solving problems		
Meeting deadlines		
Finding and correcting own errors		
Clearing up after yourself		
Helping other people		
Working as a member of a team		
Being sensitive to the needs of others		
Respecting other people's opinions		
Being tactful and discreet		
Being even-tempered		

2 Which thing from your 'difficult' list do you think you should work on improving first? Start by identifying the benefits you will gain. Then decide how to achieve your goal.

Your knowledge and skills

You already have a great deal of knowledge, as well as practical and personal skills gained at school, at home and at work (if you have a part-time job). Now you need to assess these to identify your strengths and weaknesses.

To do this accurately, try to identify evidence for your knowledge and skills. Obvious examples are:

- previous qualifications
- school reports
- occasions when you have demonstrated particular skills, such as communicating with customers or colleagues in a part-time job.

Part-time jobs give you knowledge and skills in a real work setting.

Activity: Check your skills

1 Score yourself from 1 to 5 for each of the skills in the table below.

1 = I'm very good at this skill.

2 = I'm good but could improve this skill.

3 = This skill is only average and I know that I need to improve it.

4 = I'm weak at this skill and must work hard to improve it.

5 = I've never had the chance to develop this skill.

Enter the score in the column headed 'Score A' and add today's date.

2 Look back at the units and topics you will be studying for your course – you entered them into the chart on page 10. Use this to identify any additional skills that you know are important for your course and add them to the table. Then score yourself for these skills, too.

3 Identify the main skills you will need in order to be successful in your chosen career, and highlight them in the table.

Go back and score yourself against each skill after three, six and nine months. That way you can monitor your progress and check where you need to take action to develop the most important skills you will need.

English and communication skills	Score A	Score B (after three months)	Score C (after six months)	Score D (after nine months)
Test dates:				
Reading and understanding different types of texts and information				
Speaking to other people face to face				
Speaking clearly on the telephone				
Listening carefully				
Writing clearly and concisely				
Presenting information in a logical order				
Summarising information				
Using correct punctuation and spelling				
Joining in a group discussion				
Expressing your own ideas and opinions appropriately				
Persuading other people to do something				
Making an oral presentation and presenting ideas clearly				

ICT skills	Score A	Score B (after three months)	Score C (after six months)	Score D (after nine months)
Test dates:				
Using ICT equipment correctly and safely				
Using a range of software				
Accurate keyboarding				
Proofreading				
Using the internet to find and select appropriate information				
Using ICT equipment to communicate and exchange information				
Producing professional documents which include tables and graphics				
Creating and interpreting spreadsheets				
Using PowerPoint				

Maths and numeracy skills	Score A	Score B (after three months)	Score C (after six months)	Score D (after nine months)
Test dates:				
Carrying out calculations (eg money, time, measurements etc) in a work-related situation				
Estimating amounts				
Understanding and interpreting data in tables, graphs, diagrams and charts				
Comparing prices and identifying best value for money				
Solving routine and non-routine work-related numerical problems				

Case study: Previous skills and experience

Some people decide to take a BTEC Level 2 First in Creative Media Production because they have already had some relevant experience or interest – for example, they have made a website for a club they belong to, or they are a keen photographer. Others join the course simply because they have an interest in some of the subject areas.

Some people enjoy expressing their creative side by drawing, writing or coming up with lots of ideas. Others have a more technical background and prefer to work on computers, or with cameras and lighting equipment.

Paula and Barry have both joined the BTEC Level 2 First in Creative Media Production with very different sets of interests. In different ways, they both bring skills and useful experience to the course.

Paula has always been keen on drawing and painting. She spends a lot of time at weekends sketching pictures of animals and doing portraits of her friends. She has a large collection of sketchbooks, and got a B grade in her Art GCSE. She also enjoys other crafts, such as modelling with plasticine. She likes solving problems visually and finds it very easy to do a quick sketch to demonstrate her ideas to other people.

Barry enjoys working with computers and finds it easy to learn new programs. He has always done very well in ICT at school and spends much of his spare time playing computer games. Recently he has made his own simple puzzle games on a computer using Flash. If he finds something he can't do on a computer, he likes to solve the problem on his own or by using tutorials he finds on the internet.

Are you creative and visual like Paula, or great with computers like Barry? Or a bit of both? What previous experience do you have that will help you to complete the units you are studying?

Managing your time

Some people are brilliant at managing their time. They do everything they need to and have time left over for activities they enjoy. Other people complain that they don't know where the time goes.

Which are you? If you need help to manage your time – and most people do – you will find help here.

Why time management is important

- It means you stay in control, get less stressed and don't skip important tasks.
- Some weeks will be peaceful, others will be hectic.
- The amount of homework and assignments you have to do will vary.
- As deadlines approach, time always seems to go faster.
- Some work will need to be done quickly, maybe for the next lesson; other tasks may need to be done over several days or weeks. This needs careful planning.
- You may have several assignments or tasks to complete in a short space of time.
- You want to have a social life.

Avoiding time–wasting

We can all plan to do work, and then find our plans go wrong. There may be several reasons for this. How many of the following do *you* do?

Top time-wasting activities

1	Allowing (or encouraging) people to interrupt you.
2	Not having the information, handouts or textbook you need because you've lost them or lent them to someone else.
3	Chatting to people, making calls or sending texts when you should be working.
4	Getting distracted because you simply must keep checking out MySpace, Facebook or emails.
5	Putting off jobs until they are a total nightmare, then panicking.
6	Daydreaming.
7	Making a mess of something so you have to start all over again.

Planning and getting organised

The first step in managing your time is to plan ahead and be well organised. Some people are naturally good at this. They think ahead, write down their commitments in a diary or planner, and store their notes and handouts neatly and carefully so they can find them quickly.

How good are your working habits?

Talking to friends can take up a lot of time.

Improving your planning and organisational skills

1 Use a diary or planner to schedule working times into your weekdays and weekends.

2 Have a place for everything and everything in its place.

3 Be strict with yourself when you start work. If you aren't really in the mood, set a shorter time limit and give yourself a reward when the time is up.

4 Keep a diary in which you write down exactly what work you have to do.

5 Divide up long or complex tasks into manageable chunks and put each 'chunk' in your diary with a deadline of its own.

6 Write a 'to do' list if you have several different tasks. Tick them off as you go.

7 Always allow more time than you think you need for a task.

TRY THIS

Analyse your average day.

How many hours do you spend sleeping, eating, travelling, attending school or college, working and taking part in leisure activities?

How much time is left for homework and assignments?

Case study: Getting yourself organised

When Samira started the first project of her course, her tutor explained that as part of homework all learners should write up a diary reflecting on the work they had done each day while it was still fresh in their minds.

Looking back, Samira reflects, 'For the first few weeks I kept the diary, but because I was typing it up on my computer I started to get distracted and talked to my mates on Messenger. Sometimes I'd lose track of time so the work didn't get done. I would promise myself that I'd catch up later in the week. Before I knew it, I was several sessions behind and I had to try to think back to what we had done in each session. I ended up in a panic and it took much longer than it would have done if I'd kept on top of the diary as my tutor suggested.

'After that I decided to turn over a new leaf, and for the second project my goal was to complete my diary as soon as I got home, no matter what. I got into a routine of making myself a sandwich when I got home, sitting down at my computer and getting on with it. I made sure that my Messenger service was turned off, and when I'd completed the work I'd reward myself by watching television for an hour or going round to a mate's house for a chat.

'When it came to handing the diary in, all I had to do was check though what I had written. This only took about an hour. Some other people in my class had to work all weekend before the deadline, and I ended up getting better grades for the project.'

So does Samira have any advice for anyone starting a BTEC course. 'Don't keep putting things off until another day so you end up rushing at the last minute. Find a time in your day to complete any homework tasks, such as logbook entries, and stick to it. Make it part of your routine.'

TOP TIPS

If you become distracted by social networking sites or email when you're working, set yourself a time limit of 10 minutes or so to indulge yourself.

BTEC FACT

If you have serious problems that are interfering with your ability to work or to concentrate, talk to your tutor. There are many ways in which BTEC learners who have personal difficulties can be supported to help them continue with their studies.

Activity: Managing time

1   The correct term for something you do in preference to starting a particular task is a 'displacement activity'. In the workplace this includes things like often going to the water cooler to get a drink, and constantly checking emails and so on online. People who work from home may tidy up, watch television or even cook a meal to put off starting a job.

Write down *your* top three displacement activities.

2 Today is Wednesday. Sajid has several jobs to do tonight and has started well by making a 'to do' list. He's worried that he won't get through all the things on his list and, because he works on Thursday and Friday evenings, that the rest will have to wait until Saturday.

    a) Look through Sajid's list and decide which jobs are top priority and *must* be done tonight and which can be left until Saturday if he runs out of time.

    b) Sajid is finding that his job is starting to interfere with his ability to do his assignments. What solutions can you suggest to help him?

Jobs to do

- File handouts from today's classes
- Phone Tom (left early today) to tell him the time of our presentation tomorrow has been changed to 11 am
- Research information online for next Tuesday's lesson
- Complete table from rough notes in class today
- Rewrite section of leaflet to talk about at tutorial tomorrow
- Write out class's ideas for the charity of the year, ready for course representatives meeting tomorrow lunchtime
- Redo handout Tom and I are giving out at presentation
- Plan how best to schedule assignment received today – deadline 3 weeks
- Download booklet from website ready for next Monday's class

Getting the most from work experience

On some BTEC First courses, all learners have to do a **work placement**. On others, like the BTEC Level 2 First in Creative Media Production, they are recommended but not essential. If you are doing one, you need to prepare so that you get the most out of it. The checklists in this section will help.

Before you go checklist

1. Find out about the organisation by researching online.

2. Check that you have all the information you'll need about the placement.

3. Check the route you will need to take and how long it will take you. Always allow longer on the first day.

4. Check with your tutor what clothes are suitable and make sure you look the part.

5. Check that you know any rules or guidelines you must follow.

6. Check that you know what to do if you have a serious problem during the placement, such as being too ill to go to work.

7. Talk to your tutor if you have any special personal concerns.

8. Read the unit(s) that relate to your placement carefully. Highlight points you need to remember or refer to regularly.

9. Read the assessment criteria that relate to the unit(s) and use these to make a list of the information and evidence you'll need to obtain.

10. Your tutor will give you an official logbook or diary – or just use a notebook. Make notes each evening while things are fresh in your mind, and keep them safely.

While you're on work placement

Ideally, on your first day you'll be told about the business and what you'll be expected to do. You may even be allocated to one particular member of staff who will be your 'mentor'. However, not all firms operate like this, and if everyone is very busy, your **induction** may be rushed. If so, stay positive and watch other people to see what they're doing. Then offer to help where you can.

BTEC FACT

If you need specific evidence from a work placement for a particular unit, your tutor may give you a logbook or work diary, and will tell you how you will be assessed in relation to the work that you will do.

TRY THIS

You're on work experience. The placement is interesting and related to the job you want to do. However, you've been watching people most of the time and want to get more involved. Identify three jobs you think you could offer to do.

While you're there

1 Arrive with a positive attitude, knowing that you are going to do your best and get the most out of your time there.

2 Although you may be nervous at first, don't let that stop you from smiling at people, saying 'hello' and telling them your name.

3 Arrive punctually – or even early – every day. If you're delayed for any reason, phone and explain. Then get there as soon as you can.

4 If you take your mobile phone, switch it off when you arrive.

5 If you have nothing to do, offer to help someone who is busy or ask if you can watch someone who is doing a job that interests you.

6 Always remember to thank people who give you information, show you something or agree that you can observe them.

7 If you're asked to do something and don't understand what to do, ask for it to be repeated. If it's complicated, write it down.

8 If a task is difficult, start it and then check back that you are doing it correctly before you go any further.

9 Obey all company rules, such as regulations and procedures relating to health and safety and using machinery, the use of IT equipment, and access to confidential information.

10 Don't rush off as fast as you can at the end of the day. Check first with your mentor or supervisor whether you can leave.

TOP TIPS

Observing people who are skilled at what they do helps you learn a lot, and may even be part of your **assignment brief.**

Coping with problems

Problems are rare but can happen. The most common ones are being bored because you're not given any work to do or upset because you feel someone is treating you unfairly. Normally, the best first step is to talk to your mentor at work or your supervisor. However, if you're very worried or upset, you may prefer to get in touch with your tutor instead – do it promptly.

Getting experience of work in the media

Getting work placements in the media can be difficult. Though work experience is not a mandatory part of the BTEC Level 2 First in Creative Media Production, it is recommended as it will give you a better chance of getting employment in the media sector after your studies. For this reason, some schools and colleges may insist that you undertake work experience.

You may be one of the lucky ones who is placed at a local radio station or with a web design company. However, the chances are that your school or college will not be able to secure this type of placement. There are, though, other ways of getting additional experience of working in the media while studying for your BTEC First.

If you are interested in working in radio, then a fun way of becoming familiar with all aspects of radio broadcasting is by getting involved with your local hospital radio station. If you are able to become involved, you are likely to make many new friends who share a passion for radio, and you'll be helping to provide a very valuable service. Hospital patients can gain a lot of comfort and enjoyment from listening to the broadcasts.

If you are fortunate enough to you live in an area where there are community television stations, such as Let's Go Global and Wirral TV in the North West or Southwark TV in London, find out if your local station runs youth work experience programmes. If it does, then find out how to apply for the programme.

More generally, you need to think laterally about the types of organisations that can give you experience and that can help you improve the skills you learn on your course. Many towns and villages have amateur theatrical societies that perform plays. Some groups stage performances at community centres or church halls. Others hire professional theatres. These groups often welcome technicians who can help set up the lighting or sound equipment. While this may not give you direct experience of working in television and film, it will allow you to practise your skills.

Work experience outside of the media

Work experience doesn't have to be directly related to the media to be useful. If you volunteer to work with a charity or local group, you may gain useful skills in working with people or working in a team that will look great on your CV when applying to a university or for work in a media company.

Deciding to commit

When deciding to commit to a regular undertaking, such as working with a hospital radio station or a theatre group, you will need to prove that you will be a reliable member of the team. You need to consider if you are able to make the commitments, such as being available when and where you will be needed. A radio station may need you to commit regularly once a week, say from 7–9 on Wednesday evenings, but a theatre group may need additional weekend or evening commitments during performances. You will need to make sure you can commit to the times that you have agreed and that you are able to organise the necessary travel arrangements. You will need to make sure that this does not clash with any work commitments you have on your BTEC course.

Finding a work placement or work as a volunteer

Details of organisations in your area can be found by doing an internet search. Try typing 'amateur theatre group', 'hospital radio' or 'community TV' together with the name of your town or area into a search engine.

There are several useful websites that you should access. For details, go to www.pearsonhotlinks.co.uk, insert the express code 5728S and click on the link for this page. For example, the BBC has a great work experience placement link that lists all the placements available locally within BBC television and radio. The Radio Academy has a section on its website that provides guidance about getting placements in the radio industry.

Other websites listed on the link for this page on www.pearsonhotlinks. co.uk offer good general advice on finding work experience placements and volunteer work.

Working with clients

Another way of improving your skills and getting valuable work experience is to take on projects for clients by, say, developing a website for a local group or business, or creating a music video for an up-and-coming band.

This kind of work is normally secured by word of mouth, so you may have to ask around friends and family, or contact local clubs or groups that you think may need websites or videos. You will need to consider the commitment required before agreeing to undertake any work, and agree realistic deadlines. However, if you produce work of a good standard and work within agreed deadlines, this can often lead to more work. Eventually this can can result in you building a freelance client base.

Try to list the advantages and disadvantages of undertaking work experience while completing your BTEC Level 2 First in the boxes below and opposite. One or two examples of what you might write are provided.

Advantages	Disadvantages
Meeting people of all ages who share my interest Improving my skills	Having to balance course commitments with those of the work experience

Advantages	Disadvantages

Case study: Gaining relevant experience

Georgina is in her second year of a BTEC Level 2 First in Creative Media Production. In the summer holidays before starting the course, she took part in a summer school for 14–18-year-old aspiring film-makers run by Project Livewire at an independent cinema in Manchester. She enjoyed the project so much, she has become more involved, and is now a regular contributor.

'At first I just went along with a couple of friends for something to do in the summer holidays. I'd never tried making films before, but I knew there was a video production unit on the BTEC First, so I thought it might be useful and a bit of a laugh.

'My friends dropped out after the first couple of sessions, but I really enjoyed it so I carried on going. I made new friends there too who were really keen about film-making – just being around them was a buzz, their enthusiasm was catching.

'After we'd finished the summer school I got involved in another project that meant I had to make a commitment of one night each week.

'I was a bit worried that all these outside projects would conflict with my school work, but the skills I've learned working with Project Livewire have been really useful, especially when working on the assignment for the video production unit. I found I had skills and knowledge that I could share with other people in my group. I ended up taking a leading role in my group, and I did really well in the assignment, getting a distinction.

'I've been attending Project Livewire for nearly two years now. Some of the films I've worked on have been shown in the cinema at a film festival that showcases young people's films. In September I'm planning to go on to take a BTEC Level 3 Diploma in Media, specialising in the television and film pathway.

'The management team at Project Livewire is made up of young people, so this summer I have got more involved with the running of the scheme. It is good fun, and it will look really good on a CV when I apply for university or for a job in a couple of years.'

Working with other people

Everyone finds it easy to work with people they like and far harder with those they don't. On your course you'll often be expected to work as a team to do a task. This gives you practice in working with different people.

You will be expected to:
- contribute to the task
- listen to other people's views
- adapt to other people's ways of working
- take responsibility for your own contribution
- agree the best way to resolve any problems.

These are quite complex skills. It helps if you understand the benefits to be gained by working cooperatively with other people and know the best way to achieve this.

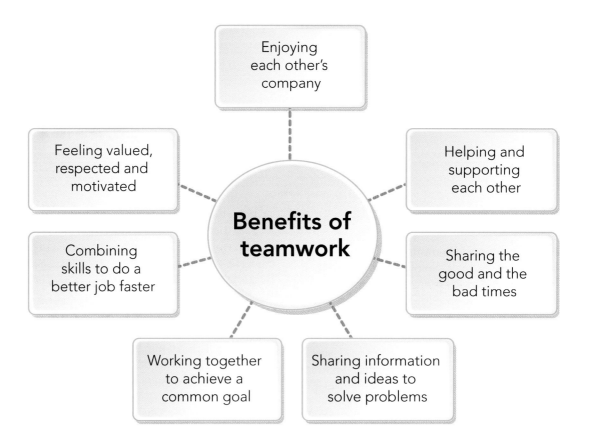

The benefits of good working relationships and teamwork

Golden rules for everyone (including the team leader!)

The secret of a successful team is that everyone works together. The role of the team leader is to make this as easy as possible by listening to people's views and coordinating everyone's efforts. A team leader is not there to give orders.

Positive teamwork checklist

✔ Be loyal to your team, including the team leader.

✔ Be reliable and dependable at all times.

✔ Be polite. Remember to say 'please' and 'thank you'.

✔ Think before you speak.

✔ Treat everyone the same.

✔ Make allowances for individual personalities. Give people 'space' if they need it, but be ready to offer support if they ask for it.

✔ Admit mistakes and apologise if you've done something wrong – learn from it but don't dwell on it.

✔ Give praise when it's due, give help when you can, and thank people who help you.

✔ Keep confidences, and any promises that you make.

Do you:

a) shrug and say nothing in case he gets upset

b) ask why he didn't text you to give you warning

c) say that it's the last time you'll ever go anywhere with him and walk off?

Which do you think would be the most effective – and why?

TRY THIS

Work out whether you're usually passive, assertive or aggressive when you're annoyed. You've arranged to meet Sam to see a film. He arrives 20 minutes late.

Teamwork

Many people who earn a living in the media work as part of a team. During many of the projects you will complete on your BTEC Level 2 First in Creative Media Production you will be required to work in a team. For example, when working on the production of a video, whether professionally or as part of an assignment, the team might include individual members who take on the roles of production manager, camera operator, lighting technician etc.

This is how a group of learners at a school in Surrey went about the teamwork aspects of a video production project. They visited a small production company and met the in-house team. On returning to school, their tutor asked the learners to formalise their work as a team by organising themselves as a video production company and by writing down the rules and the responsibilities of each member.

○ The group drew up a list of aims and objectives. For example, they noted that the company's aim was to create a promotional video for the school.

○ They compiled a list of ground rules setting out what was expected of team members. This included a requirement to turn up on time for production planning meetings and video shoots.

○ They drew up a list of rules for team meetings to ensure that their time was used productively. These rules included not eating or using mobile phones in meetings or when filming, respecting other people's opinions, and not arguing or interrupting when other people are talking.

○ They decided that the job of chairing the team meetings and the job of taking the minutes should be taken by different team members at each meeting. These jobs would switch between members on a rotating basis.

○ They agreed who would undertake the various roles in the project, and drafted a separate 'contract' for each team member, setting out that person's roles and responsibilities. Each member signed their contract.

○ The group attached copies of the contracts to the wall of the room they used as their production base.

There are many benefits to be gained from working as a team.

Do you think the activities listed on the previous page will help the group work together as a team during their video production project?

Teamwork during projects

During the course you might work as a team on several projects, but let's take a look in a little more detail at how a team works during a project that covers aspects of the video production and advertising production units.

A team of learners has been asked to produce a television advert for a new children's toy. Before committing to filming, the team will need to hold meetings to come up with many different ideas for the advert. They must decide which ideas to develop, and then plan the video, talk about resources and budget, and allocate roles to each team member. It is essential that there is a supportive atmosphere in these meetings. Team members must respect each other. They must feel that they can present their ideas and opinions without being laughed at or ridiculed.

Good communication is vital during meetings to ensure decisions are clearly understood and the project progresses as it should. When taking part in meetings, it is important that team members express themselves clearly while also taking the views and feelings of others into consideration.

This consideration should also be shown in conversations. The learners wrote down their initial ideas in marker pen on large sheets of paper and pinned them up on the wall for others to discuss. When looking at the ideas put forward by one student, another member of the group said, 'Your ideas are stupid. I'll bet everyone here thinks they're rubbish.'

What might the effect of this comment be on:
a) the learner whose idea was being discussed

b) the others in the group?

If you think an idea is not right for a project, it is important that you say so. However, you must try and provide constructive feedback rather than just saying that something is stupid or rubbish.

For example, another way of communicating concern over the ideas for the children's toy advert might have been to say, 'You've come up with some good ideas, but I'm not sure they're right for the age group we're aiming the advert at. Children have short attention spans, and they might get bored and stop watching unless we do something that they'll find a bit more exciting.'

You often need to think about the best way of giving feedback. Consider the statements below and suggest a more appropriate comment in each case.

What was said...	How it might have been said...
'This is just the same as the last set of ideas you came up with. You haven't even tried.'	
'My ideas for the documentary are way better than yours.'	
'Why can't you be quiet and let someone else speak?'	
'This is the first time you've been here in weeks. I don't see why we should listen to you.'	

Come up with three golden rules for supporting other members of the group during meetings.

1

2

3

Taking part in a video shoot is hard work. Whether working in a studio or on location, it is vital that concentration and focus are maintained throughout. Behaviour such as chatting or texting can be distracting and may waste valuable time.

Come up with three golden rules for good behaviour when working on a video shoot in a studio.

1

2

3

Getting the most from special events

BTEC First courses usually include several practical activities and special events. These enable you to find out information, develop your skills and knowledge in new situations, and enjoy new experiences. They may include visits to external venues, visits from specialist speakers, and team events.

You may be able to visit a TV studio to observe filming.

Most learners enjoy the chance to do something different. You'll probably look forward to some events more than others. If you're ready to get actively involved, you'll usually gain the most benefit. It also helps to make a few preparations!

Case study: A visit to a museum

Alex visited the National Museum of Media in Bradford with other learners on the BTEC Level 2 First in Creative Media Production. Here are Alex's observations on the visit.

'I wasn't too keen on going to the Museum of Media beforehand. I've always thought of museums as boring dusty places for old people. When we arrived at the museum I was really surprised at how much there is to do and how exiting it all appears.

'First we went into the television studio. It was great to see the real equipment that professionals actually use. We could even have a go at operating the cameras. The big blue 'chroma' screen is great, we could stand in front of it and the television alongside would show us in different 'locations', such as outside Downing Street or on a flying carpet. We then watched a short animated 3D film about dinosaurs at the Imax cinema.

'After this we had some free time to look at the rest of the museum. There is an exhibition of photography and an area which explores photography through the ages. I do some photography in my spare time so I found this really interesting.

'The animation area has many models and drawings that have been used on well-known animations, including some of the original models used for Wallace and Gromit films. You can also play with different methods of animation such as thaumatropes. The best bit was that we got to watch a professional animator working with models on a stop-frame animation.

'When we got back our tutor asked us to write a diary of the day, and to try to think how the things we did and saw at the museum might help us with the units we are studying on the course. I thought of three areas straightaway: animation techniques, video production and photography techniques. I think the visit to the museum really helped bring the things we are studying to life.'

Special events checklist

✔ Check you understand how the event relates to your course.

✔ If a visit or trip is not something you would normally find very interesting, try to keep an open mind. You might get a surprise!

✔ Find out what you're expected to do, and any rules or guidelines you must follow, including about your clothes or appearance.

✔ Always allow enough time to arrive five minutes early, and make sure you're never late.

✔ On an external visit, make notes on what you see and hear. This is essential if you have to write about it afterwards, use your information to answer questions in an assignment or do something practical.

✔ If an external speaker is going to talk to your class, prepare a list of questions in advance. Nominate someone to thank the speaker afterwards. If you want to record the talk, it's polite to ask first.

✔ For a team event, you may be involved in planning and helping to allocate different team roles. You'll be expected to participate positively in any discussions, to talk for some (but not all) of the time, and perhaps to volunteer for some jobs yourself.

✔ Write up any notes you make as soon as you can – while you can still understand what you wrote!

TRY THIS

At the last minute, you're asked to propose a vote of thanks to a visiting speaker on behalf of your class. What would you say?

Resources and research

Understanding resources

Resources are items that help you do something. The most obvious one is money! To obtain your BTEC First award, however, your resources are rather different.

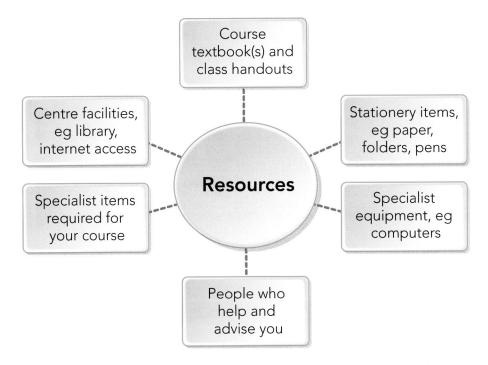

Different kinds of resources

Physical resources

Physical resources are things like textbooks, computers and any specialist equipment.

- Popular textbooks, laptops for home use and specialist equipment may need to be booked. Leaving it until the last minute is risky.

- You can ask for help if you don't know how to use resources properly.

- You should check what stationery and equipment you need at the start of your course and make sure you have it.

- You need to look after your resources carefully. This saves money and time spent replacing lost items.

People as resources

There are many people who can help you through your course:

- family members who help and support you

- your tutor

○ friends in your group who collect handouts for you and phone you to keep you up to date when you're absent

○ librarians and computer technicians at your centre or your local library

○ expert practitioners.

Expert practitioners

Expert practitioners have worked hard to be successful in their chosen area. They have the skills and knowledge needed to do the job properly. They can be invaluable when you're researching information (see page 51). You can also learn a lot by watching them at work, especially if you can ask them questions about what they do, what they find hard, and any difficulties they've had.

Talking to a radio presenter will give you insights into what happens behind the scenes.

Try to observe more than one expert practitioner:

○ It gives you a better picture about what they do.

○ No single job will cover all aspects of work that might apply to your studies.

○ You may find some experts more approachable and easy to understand than others. For example, if someone is impatient because they're busy it may be difficult to ask them questions, or if someone works very quickly you may find it hard to follow what they're doing.

If you have problems, just note what you've learned and compare it with your other observations. And there's always the chance that you're observing someone who's not very good at their job! You'll only know this for certain if you've seen what people should be doing.

Preparing for a visit

During your BTEC Level 2 First in Creative Media Production you may undertake several visits and excursions. For example, you could tour around professional places of work, such as TV studios where you might get the opportunity to talk to people working in the industry. Your tutor might also invite professionals to visit your class as a guest speaker.

Preparing to meet industry professionals

Before meeting professionals working in the media, whether they are visiting as a guest speaker or whether you are visiting their place of work, it is a good idea to find out about about the particular media industry they work in and the organisation they work for. You can do some research on the internet. Here are a list of questions you could research.

- What media industry is the company involved in?
- Who are the company's main customers?
- How many people does the company employ?
- Is the company local, national or multinational?
- Who owns the company – is it privately owned, part of a bigger group of companies or a public company?
- What sort of job roles are there within the company?

The grid below can be used to make notes before a visit or a meeting.

Media industry	What industry (or industries) is the company involved in?
	Who are the company's main customers and what work are they most well known for?
Size and profile	How many people does the company employ?
	Is the company local, national or multinational?
Ownership	Who owns the company? Is it privately owned, part of a bigger group of companies or a public company?
Job roles	What sort of job roles are there within the company?

Use this space to record any other useful information you find out	

You should also put together a list of questions that you would like to ask during the visit. Of course, you could ask any of the questions you were unable to answer in your research before the meeting. However, also think what aspects of the company or the individual's job you might find particularly interesting, or what information might be useful to your assignment work. You could, for example, ask these questions if you have the chance to speak to a professional working in the media.

- What is your job role? What do you do on a normal working day?
- Do you work on your own or as part of a team? What roles do other team members do?
- What sort of hours do you work?
- Are you a full-time employee or do you work freelance or on short-term contracts? Are you salaried, paid by the hour, or paid on completion of a contract?
- What technical skills are required to do this job?
- What personal qualities are important to do the job?
- What qualifications are important to get this type of job?
- What opportunities are there for people starting out in this part of the media?
- How did you apply for this job and how are jobs like this normally advertised?

The grid on pages 43 and 44 can be used to make a list of your questions and to take notes about the answers you get.

Meeting with (industry professional's name): From (company's name): Date:	
Job roles and conditions	What is your job role? What do you do on a normal working day? Do you work on your own or as part of a team? What roles do other team members do? What sort of hours do you work? Employment status: full-time employee, freelance or short-term contract? Pay: salaried, paid by the hour, or paid on completion of a contract?
Skills and qualities	What technical skills are required to do this job? What personal qualities are important to do this job? What qualifications are important to get this type of job?

Opportunities	What opportunities are there for young people starting out in this industry?
	How did you apply for your job and how are jobs like yours normally advertised?
Use this space to note any other questions you might wish to ask or to record useful information you find out	

Create your own resource list

On a BTEC Level 2 First in Creative Media Production, you will draw on the knowledge and skills of tutors and of each other when completing the projects and assignments that you will be set. However, you will also need to use a range of physical resources and equipment to complete your course.

Library-based resources

Books and magazines will be a valuable resource when undertaking research. Whether you are researching for a presentation about different printing techniques or finding out about which genres of television programme appeal to particular types of audience, books and magazines will be a valuable resource.

Internet resources

Websites can be a valuable source of information when researching the work of practitioners. The websites of many media production companies have detailed information about how they were formed, the work they do and the way in which they are managed and funded. Other sites not only have useful industry information but activities you can have a go at which will help you learn.

Be careful of relying on Wikipedia or on what people say on blog sites, as it isn't always correct. If you are not sure about information, always check it using several sources, and if you use information from the internet in your work always make a note of where you got it from and try to put your understanding of the information in your own words.

Stationery

Much of the work you will undertake on the course is practical. To record your ideas and to make notes in class or when undertaking visits, you will need sketchbooks and notebooks. You should always make sure you are equipped with pens and pencils, along with a file to keep handouts, notes and work you complete for homework tasks.

Other equipment

Some units may require you to have access to specific equipment. Most of this equipment will be provided by your school or college, but you may need some items of personal equipment. For example, if you have a computer you can use at home, it may be useful to have a USB drive so that you can copy work you have done on school or college computers and work more on it at home.

You are unlikely to be required to own a digital camera or video camera for the photography techniques or video production units. However, if you do have one you can use it to do additional work in your own time.

A personal resource list

Use the grid on the next page to create your own resource list. Your tutor may suggest items that should be included for the units you are studying.

Your tutor may also provide a reading list of useful books and magazines, or you could visit your school or college library to gather information about relevant books you may need to refer to on your course.

Library-based resources, such as books and magazines
Internet resources
Stationery
Equipment that you have which may be useful, such as computers and cameras
Other equipment that would be useful

Finding the information you need

The information explosion

There are lots of different ways to find out information – books, newspapers, magazines, television, radio, CDs, DVDs, the internet. And you can exchange information with other people by texting, sending an email or phoning someone.

All this makes it much easier to obtain information. If you know what you're doing, you can probably find most of what you need sitting at a computer. But there are some dangers:

- Finding exactly what you want online takes skill. You need to know what you're doing.
- It's easy to get too much information and become overwhelmed.
- It's unlikely that everything you need will be available online.
- The information you read may be out of date.
- The information may be neither reliable nor true.

Define what you are trying to find. (The more precise you are, the more likely you are to find what you're looking for.)

Know where to look for it. (Remember: the internet is not the only source of information.)

Recognise when you have found appropriate information.

Know what to do with information once you've found it. (Make sure that you understand it, interpret it correctly and record the source where you found it.)

Know when to stop looking (especially if you have a deadline).

Finding and using information effectively

Before you start

There are four things that will help you look in the right place and target your search properly.

Ask yourself ...	Because ...	Example
Exactly what do I need to find out?	It will save you time and effort.	If you need information about accidents, you need to know what type of accident and over what time period.
Why do I need this information and who is going to read it?	This puts the task into context. You need to identify the best type of information to obtain and how to get it.	If you're making a poster or leaflet for children, you'll need simple information that can be presented in a graphical format. If, however, you're giving a workplace presentation on accidents, you'll need tables and graphs to illustrate your talk.
Where can I find it?	You need to consider whether your source is trustworthy and up to date. The internet is great, but you must check that the sites you use are reliable.	To find out about accidents in the workplace you could talk to the health and safety at work officer. To find examples of accidents in your local area you could look through back copies of your local newspaper in the local library or newspaper offices.
What is my deadline?	You know how long you have to find the information and use it.	

TRY THIS

Schedule your research time by calculating backwards from the deadline date. Split the time you have 50/50 between searching for information and using it. This stops you searching for too long and getting lots of interesting material, but then not having the time to use it properly!

Your three main sources of information are:
- libraries or learning resource centres
- the internet
- asking other people, for example through interviews and questionnaires.

Researching in libraries

You can use the learning resource centre in your school or college, or a local public library. Public libraries usually have a large reference section with many resources available for loan, including CD-ROMs, encyclopaedias, government statistics, magazines, journals and newspapers, and databases such as Infotrac, which contains articles from newspapers and magazines over the last five years.

The librarian will show you how to find the resources you need and how to look up a specific book (or author) to check if it is available or is out on loan.

Some books and resources can only be used in the library itself, while others can be taken out on short-term or long-term loan. You need to plan how to access and use the resources that are popular or restricted.

Using your library

✔ If your centre has an intranet you might be able to check which books and CD-ROMs are available without actually visiting the library.

✔ All libraries have photocopying facilities, so take enough change with you to copy articles that you can't remove. Write down the source of any article you photocopy, ie the name and the date of the publication.

✔ Learn how to keep a reference file (or bibliography) in which you store the details of all your sources and references. A bibliography must include CDs, DVDs and other information formats, not just books and magazines.

✔ If your search is complicated, go at a quiet time when the librarian can help you.

✔ Don't get carried away if you find several books that contain the information you need. Too many can be confusing.

✔ Use the index to find information quickly by searching for key words. Scan the index using several likely alternatives.

✔ Only use books that you find easy to understand. A book is only helpful if you can retell the information in your own words.

Researching online

A good search engine such as Google will help you find useful websites. They look for sites based on the information you enter in the search box. In some cases, such as Ask.co.uk, you may get the chance to refine your choice after entering your key words or question.

Finding information on a website

Wikipedia is a popular free online encyclopaedia. It has been criticised because entries may be inaccurate as members of the public can edit the site. However, Wikipedia is trying to prevent this by organising professional editing.

If you're not sure whether something you read is correct, or if there is anything strange about it, check it against information on another site. Make sure you ask your tutor's opinion, too.

With large websites, it can be difficult to find what you need. Always read the whole screen – there may be several menus in different parts of the screen.

To help you search, many large websites have:

- their own search facility or a site map that lists site content with links to the different pages
- links to similar sites where you might find more information. Clicking a link should open a new window, so you'll still be connected to the original site.

TRY THIS

Search engines don't just find websites. On Google, the options at the top of your screen include 'images', 'news' and 'maps'. If you click on 'more' and then 'even more', you'll find other options, too. You'll usually find the most relevant information if you use the UK version of a search engine. Only search the whole web if you deliberately want to include European and American information. To see this in action, go to www.pearsonhotlinks.co.uk, insert the express code 5728S and click on the link for this page.

There may be useful information and links at the top, foot or either side of a web page.

There are several other useful sites you could visit when researching online.

- **Directory sites** show websites in specific categories so you can focus your search at the start.

- **Forums** are sites, or areas of a website, where people post comments on an issue. They can be useful if you want to find out opinions on a topic. You can usually read them without registering.

- **News sites** include the BBC website as well as the sites for all the daily newspapers. Check the website of your local newspaper, too.

Printing information

- Only print information that you're sure will be useful. It's easy to print too much and find yourself drowning in paper.

- Make quick notes on your print-outs so that you remember why you wanted them. It will jog your memory when you're sorting through them later.

- If there's a printer-friendly option, use it. It will give you a print-out without unnecessary graphics or adverts.

- Check the bottom line of your print-outs. It should show the URL for that page of the website, and the date. You need those if you have to list your sources or if you want to quote from the page.

Researching by asking other people

You're likely to do this for two reasons:

- you need help from someone who knows a lot about a topic

- you need to find out several people's opinions on something.

TRY THIS

To see how directory sites work go to www.pearsonhotlinks.co.uk, insert the express code 5728S and click on the link for this page.

TOP TIPS

Bookmark sites you use regularly by adding the URL to your browser. How to do this will depend on which browser you use, eg Internet Explorer, Firefox.

Information from an expert

Explain politely why you are carrying out the investigation. Ask questions slowly and clearly about what they do and how they do it. If they don't mind, you could take written notes so you remember what they tell you. Put the name and title of the person, and the date, at the top. This is especially important if you might be seeing more than one person, to avoid getting your notes muddled up.

Ask whether you may contact them again, in case there's anything you need to check. Write down their phone number or email address. Above all, remember to say 'thank you'!

Case study: A games project

On a BTEC Level 2 First in Creative Media Production, you can carry out research for many reasons. You might look at specific areas of the industry or particular jobs, you might find out more about historical techniques, or research content for an article or website.

Some of the research you will undertake will be done on your own and some will be carried out in groups with the results shared with the whole team.

A group from Little Upton High School is working on a project to produce a proposal for a computer game aimed at 14–16-year-olds. The assignment links to Unit 1: Research for Media Production. To put together the proposal, the students need to understand more about the sort of computer games that appeal to their target audience. This will involve different research tasks, which the students share out across the team.

Joe and Stephanie undertake an investigation into the most popular games for the target market by searching the internet for relevant sales statistics. They also go onto games chat rooms, forums and games review sites to find out what people are saying about the games that sell well to this age group.

Andrew and Jahni investigate which games sell well locally. They obtain sales trends by interviewing the store managers at two local computer games stores. Before conducting the interviews, they draw up a list of questions that they need to ask.

Ahmad and Katrina put together a questionnaire which they give to several 14–16-year-olds. This is designed to find out what type of games they like to play and why.

When the team has completed this research, they come up with three ideas for a game. To help them finalise which idea they are going to take into the production stage, they present all three proposals to a 'focus group' of 12 other 14–16-year-olds. They listen closely to see which idea is most popular, noting any differences in opinion between the boys and girls in the focus group.

The opinions of several people

The easiest way to do this is with a questionnaire. You can either give people the questionnaire to complete themselves, or interview them and complete it yourself. Professional interviewers often telephone people to ask questions, but at this stage it's not a good idea unless you know the people you're phoning and they're happy for you to do this.

Devising a questionnaire

1 Make sure it has a title and clear instructions.

2 Rather than ask for opinions, give people options, eg yes/no, maybe/always, never/sometimes. This will make it easier to analyse the results.

3 Or you can ask interviewees to give a score, say out of 5, making it clear what each number represents, eg 5 = excellent, 3 = very good.

4 Keep your questionnaire short so that your interviewees don't lose interest. Between 10 and 15 questions is probably about right, as long as that's enough to find out all you need.

5 Remember to add 'thank you' at the end.

6 Decide upon the representative sample of people you will approach. These are the people whose views are the most relevant to the topic you're investigating.

7 Decide how many responses you need to get a valid answer. This means that the answer is representative of the wider population. For example, if you want views on food in your canteen, it's pointless only asking five people. You might pick the only five people who detest (or love) the food it serves.

Keeping a logbook

A reflective logbook is a good way of compiling reseach information. This could include notes taken in classes, ideas, sketches, analysis of any research you have done, notes taken during meetings and records showing the different stages of any project you are undertaking. If you are required to keep a log for a unit, make sure that you complete it regularly while the work you have undertaken is still fresh in your mind.

This is an extract from a process log produced by a student taking the photography techniques unit as a part of his BTEC First.

Lyle Barker – Reflective log, Thursday 6 May
Summary of work undertaken in the last session
This week was the first session and we looked at a few different styles and uses of photography, such as fashion, portraits, documentary. We looked through some books and magazines and tried to identify the reasons different photos had been taken, such as to advertise stuff, to document a news story etc.
What we did for homework
For homework we were asked to find some photographs that we really liked. I found some portraits by a photographer called Steve McCurry. I really liked one where he had taken a picture of an Afghan girl and then taken another picture of her 15 years later, you could tell it was the same lady by the very green eyes.
What needs to be done next?
We have to come up with ideas for our own photographs. I'd like to do a pair of portraits like Steve McCurry, but obviously I can't wait 15 years for someone to change!
I think I'd like to take a picture of my sister who is twelve and a picture of my mum in the same position, and try to get it so people can see that they look a bit alike.

Lyle's log is good because he doesn't simply describe his research, he says what he likes about the photographs he has researched and how he can relate these to his own ideas. Later in the log he reflects on the work he has done, and includes some suggestions for improvement and development.

> I came up with my idea really quickly and I thought it was a good one. Looking back now, I wish I'd come up with a few more good ideas but I still like the one that I used.
>
> The photographs were easy to set up as the models are members of my family. Both my sister and mum posed really well, and they really look similar to each other. My sister got the giggles, so I had to take several photographs to get it right. I can see what it must be like for professional photographers and the difficulties they have to put up with.
>
> If I have to take similar pictures again, I would get my mum and sister in the studio at college so I could get the lighting right. I would help to choose the colours of clothes they would be wearing so that they would look just right against the coloured backdrop.

Activity: Keeping a research log

If you are completing a project that involves research, it is a good idea to keep a research log that:

- lists the resources you used and the materials you looked at
- states when and where you found each resource, and where relevant details how one source led to another
- sums up very briefly what was learnt from each resource.

This is an extract from the research log of Daniel, who is researching the job role of camera operator. He has got the opportunity of interviewing Jim, a professional camera operator, on a visit to a local television studio.

Name: Daniel Herstell

Assignment: Job roles in the creative media industry

Source/ material	When and where found	How found	Brief summary of information gathered	Comments
Wikipedia	en.wikipedia.org/ wiki/Camera_ operator Visited 20/09/09	Internet search	General overview of the duties of a camera operator.	Useful links at bottom to other roles in televison and film production.
Skillset	www.skillset.org/ film/jobs/camera/ article_4688_1. asp	Website recommended by tutor	More info on the duties of a camera operator.	Good for checking and expanding on info from Wikipedia. Good downloadable fact sheet.

Name: Daniel Herstell

Assignment: Job roles in the creative media industry

Source/ material	When and where found	How found	Brief summary of information gathered	Comments
Fact sheet: Camera operator	www.skillset.org/ uploads/pdfasset_ 7239.pdf?2	Downloadable pdf link from Skillset	Detailed article that gives information on the work, knowledge and skills, and career routes.	Includes some other leads to check out, like the British Society of Cinematographers.
Interview with Jim Palmer, camera operator for Channel M	Visit to Channel M, 29/9/09	Visit arranged by our tutor	Day-to-day duties during studio and location filming. Working conditions, and qualifications and skills needed. Best and worst things about the job.	Really good to speak to someone in person. I felt like I got a real sense of what it is like to do the job.

Use the blank log sheet below to research a job role in the media sector that you are interested in for a future career.

Name:

Activity: Future career research

Source/ material	When and where found	How found	Brief summary of information gathered	Comments

Managing your information

Whether you've found lots of information or only a little, assessing what you have and using it wisely is very important. This section will help you avoid the main pitfalls.

Organising and selecting your information

Organising your information

The first step is to organise your information so that it's easy to use.

- Make sure your written notes are neat and have a clear heading – it's often useful to date them, too.
- Note useful pages in any books or magazines you have borrowed.
- Highlight relevant parts of any handouts or leaflets.
- Work out the results of any questionnaires you've used.

Selecting your information

Re-read the **assignment brief** or instructions you were given, to remind yourself of the exact wording of the question(s) and divide your information into three groups:

1 Information that is totally relevant.

2 Information that is not as good, but could come in useful.

3 Information that doesn't match the questions or assignment brief very much but that you kept because you couldn't find anything better!

Check there are no obvious gaps in your information against the questions or assignment brief. If there are, make a note of them so that you know exactly what you still have to find. Although it's ideal to have everything you need before you start work, don't delay if you're short of time.

Putting your information in order

Putting your information in a logical order means you can find what you want easily. It will save you time in the long run. This is doubly important if you have lots of information and will be doing the work over several sessions.

Case study: Organising your research

Craig is working on an advertising production project.

'This term we have been studying advertising. We have had to find out about different advertising techniques by looking at hundreds of adverts for different products. We then had to come up with ideas for advertising a new mobile phone using some of the techniques and styles we researched. After coming up with some initial ideas, we have been working in teams to decide which ideas should be developed into final adverts.

'At the beginning of the project our tutor told us to use a folder to organise the information we would gather and to record the ideas we would explore and develop during the project.

'I divided my folder into three main sections.

- Research on adverts
  We had to collect examples of different styles of adverts, and then annotate them to explain the techniques they use to encourage the target market to buy the products.

- Ideas
  I kept a notebook to sketch and reord the ideas I came up with, and to explain the different techniques I tried to use.

- Meeting diary
  I kept a note of what we discussed during the meetings we held as a team. I talked about the reasons for the decisions we made when choosing ideas for the final advert.

'Setting up my folder the way our tutor suggested has really helped me to organise all the information I have found and used during the project. It's really beginning to fill up now. At first, I only looked at existing adverts for mobile phones but once I started coming up with ideas I found examples of adverts for many other products that use similar techniques. I'm really enjoying adding to it each session.'

Activity: Exploring ideas

In your project work for the BTEC Level 2 First in Creative Media Production you will often need to develop ideas. Whether you are coming up with ideas for an advertisement or an animation, you will need to find a way of organising these ideas. You will need to keep a record of any research you undertake to develop these ideas. You will also need to keep a note of these ideas in your log, or sometimes to present them to your fellow learners. A good way of doing this is to use a mind map or spidergram.

The diagram at the top of the opposite page shows how this can be done. This has been produced by Alan, Shami and Abdullah, students at Little Upton High School. As part of their studies on Unit 4: Media Audiences and Products, they have been asked to jot down different genres of film and television programmes. They have been told to think about sub-genres and the factors that might go to make up each genre.

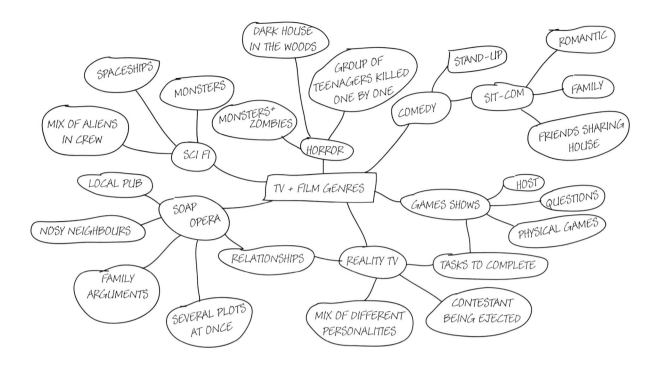

Try using the spidergram below to collate the information you have gathered about the BTEC First in Creative Media Production.

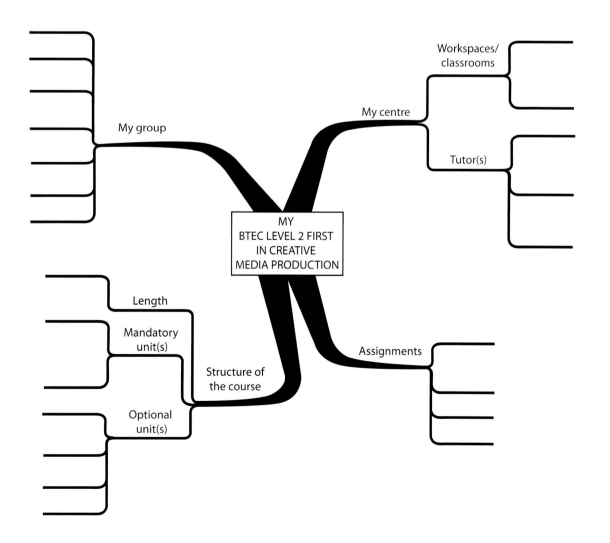

Interpreting and presenting your information

The next stage is to use your information to prepare the document and/or oral presentation you have to give. There are four steps:

1 Understand what you're reading.

2 Interpret what you're reading.

3 Know the best form in which to produce the information, bearing in mind the purpose for which it is required.

4 Create the required document so that it's in a suitable layout with correct spelling and punctuation.

Understanding what you read

As a general rule, never use information that you don't understand. However, nobody understands complex or unfamiliar material the first time they read it, especially if they just scan through it quickly. Before you reject it, try this:

Read it once to get the main idea.	Read it again, slowly, to try to take in more detail.	Look up any words you don't know in a dictionary to find out what they mean.
Write your own version.	Summarise the main points in your own words.	Read it a third time and underline or highlight the main points. (If this is a book or magazine that you shouldn't write in, take a photocopy first and write on that.)

Special note: Show both the article and your own version to your tutor to check your understanding. This will help you identify any points you missed out and help you improve your skills of interpreting and summarising.

Understanding unfamiliar information

BTEC FACT

In your assignments, it's better to separate opinions from facts. If you're quoting someone's views, make this clear. (See also page 60.)

Interpreting what you read

Interpreting what you read is different from understanding it. This is because you can't always take it for granted that something you read means what it says. The writer may have had a very strong or biased opinion, or may have exaggerated for effect. This doesn't mean that you can't use the information.

Strong opinions and bias

People often have strong points of view about certain topics. This may be based on reliable facts, but not always! We can all jump to conclusions that may not be very logical, especially if we feel strongly about something.

Things aren't always what they seem to be. Are these boys fighting or are they having a good time?

Exaggeration

Many newspapers exaggerate facts to startle and attract their readers.

LOCAL FIRM DOUBLES STAFF IN TWO WEEKS!

This newspaper headline sounds very positive. You could easily think it means employment is growing and there are more jobs in your area. Then you read on, and find the firm had only four staff and now has eight!

Tables and graphs

You need to be able to interpret what the figures mean, especially when you look at differences between columns or rows. For example, your friend might have an impressive spreadsheet that lists his income and expenditure. In reality, it doesn't tell you much until you add the figures up and subtract one from the other. Only then can you say whether he is getting into debt. And even if he is, you need to see his budget over a few months, rather than just one which may be exceptional.

Choosing a format

You may have been given specific instructions about the format and layout of a document you have to produce, in which case life is easy as long as you follow them! If not, think carefully about the best way to set out your information so that it is clear.

TRY THIS

There are many scare stories in the media about issues such as immigration, children's reading ability or obesity. Next time you're watching television and these are discussed, see if you can spot biased views, exaggeration and claims without any supporting evidence.

TOP TIPS

Never make assumptions or jump to conclusions. Make sure you have all the evidence to support your views.

Different formats	Example
text	when you write in paragraphs or prepare a report or summary
graphical	a diagram, graph or chart
pictorial	a drawing, photograph, cartoon or pictogram
tabular	numerical information in a table

The best method(s) will depend on the information you have, the source(s) of your material and the purpose of the document – a leaflet for schoolchildren needs graphics and pictures to make it lively, whereas a report to company shareholders would be mainly in text form with just one or two graphs.

Stating your sources

Whatever format you use, if you are including other people's views, comments or opinions, or copying a table or diagram from another publication, you must state the source by including the name of the author, publication or the web address. This can be in the text or as part of a list at the end. Failure to do this (so you are really pretending other people's work is your own) is known as **plagiarism**. It is a serious offence with penalties to match.

Text format

Creating written documents gets easier with practice. These points should help.

TOP TIPS

Don't just rely on your spellchecker. It won't find a word spelled wrongly that makes another valid word (eg from/form), so you must proofread everything. And remember to check whether it is set to check American English or British English. There are some spelling differences.

Golden rules for written documents

1. Think about who will be reading it, then write in an appropriate language and style.

2. Ensure it is technically correct, ie no wrong spellings or bad punctuation.

3. Take time to make it look good, with clear headings, consistent spacing and plenty of white space.

4. Write in paragraphs, each with a different theme. Leave a line space between each one.

5. If you have a lot of separate points to mention, use bullets or numbered points. Numbered points show a certain order or quantity (step 1, step 2, etc). Use bullet points when there is no suggested order.

6. Only use words that you understand the meaning of, or it might look as if you don't know what you mean.

7. Structure your document so that it has a beginning, middle and end.

8. Prepare a draft and ask your tutor to confirm you are on the right track and are using your information in the best way.

Graphical format

← **TRY THIS**

Someone asks for directions to your house. Would you write a list or draw a diagram? Which would be easier for you and for the other person – and why?

Most people find graphics better than a long description for creating a quick picture in the viewer's mind. There are several types of graphical format, and you can easily produce any of these if you have good ICT skills.

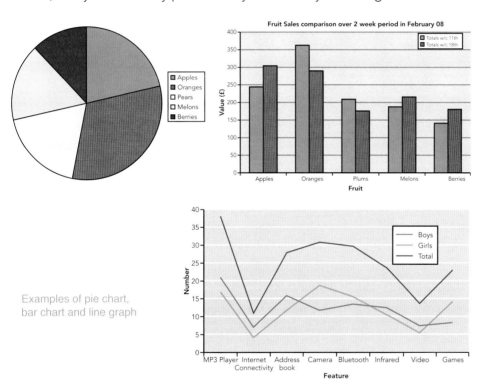

Examples of pie chart, bar chart and line graph

Pictorial format

Newspapers and magazines use pictures to illustrate situations and reduce the amount of words needed. It doesn't always have to be photographs though. For example, a new building may be sketched to show what it will look like.

A pictogram or pictograph is another type of pictorial format, such as charts which use the image of an object (fruit, coins, even pizzas) to represent data, such as the number eaten or amount spent.

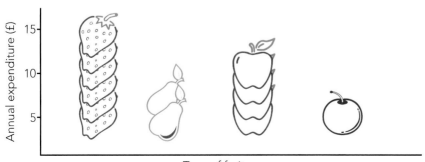

TOP TIPS

Don't spend hours writing text when an illustration can do the job better – but make sure the illustration you choose is suitable for the document and the reader.

Tabular format

A table can be an easy way to communicate information. Imagine a retailer preparing information about the items in stock. Text would be difficult to understand, and comparisons between stock levels and sales would be almost impossible to make. A table, however, would easily show the fastest-selling items.

Tables are also ideal if you are showing rankings – such as best-selling music or books.

Bestsellers list – September 2009

Position	Title	Author	Imprint	Publication
1 (New)	Lost Symbol,The	Brown, Dan	Bantam Press	15-Sep-2009
2 (1)	Complaints, The	Rankin, Ian	Orion	03-Sep-2009
3 (New)	Return Journey, The	Binchy, Maeve	Orion	17-Sep-2009
4 (7)	Sapphire	Price, Katie	Century	30-Jul-2009
5 (9)	Wolf Hall	Mantel, Hilary	Fourth Estate	30-Apr-2009
6 (3)	Week in December, A	Faulks, Sebastian	Hutchinson	03-Sep-2009
7 (2	Alex Cross's Trial	Patterson, James	Century	10-Sep-2009
8 (4)	White Queen, The	Gregory, Philippa	Simon & Schuster Ltd	18-Aug-2009
9 (5)	Even Money	Francis, Dick & Francis, Felix	Michael Joseph	03-Sep-2009
10 (8)	206 Bones	Reichs, Kathy	William Heinemann	27-Aug-2009

National newspaper circulation – September 2009

	August 2009	August 2008	% change on last year	August 09 (without bulks)	March 2009 – August 2009	% change on last year
Sun	3,128,501	3,148,792	-0.64	3,128,501	3,052,480	-2.25
Daily Mail	2,171,686	2,258,843	-3.86	2,044,079	2,178,462	-4.45
Daily Mirror	1,324,883	1,455,270	-8.96	1,324,883	1,331,108	9.44
Daily Star	886,814	751,494	18.01	886,814	855,511	16.65
The Daily Telegraph	814,087	860,298	-5.37	722,644	807,328	-6.73
Daily Express	730,234	748,664	-2.46	730,234	727,824	-1.32
Times	576,185	612,779	-5.97	529,746	588,471	-4.63
Financial Times	395,845	417,570	-5.2	365,269	411,098	-6.7
Daily Record	347,302	390,197	-10.99	345,277	350,306	-10.59
Guardian	311,387	332,587	-6.37	311,387	332,790	-4.11
Independent	187,837	230,033	-18.34	148,551	198,445	-16.76

Activity: Choosing an appropriate format

You will need to present a variety of information for many different reasons during your BTEC First. The table below lists different types of information in the first column. In the second column, state the type of format you think would be best for presenting that information. Give reasons for your choices. Choose from

- text format
- graphical format (including mind maps)
- pictorial format
- tabular format.

Type of information	Format
The results of a survey about which genre of film or game a particular target audience prefers	
Information gathered about the development of technology for games or animation	
Ideas for a character design for a game or animation	
Showing the ideas for an advertisement which have been generated during a team meeting, and explaining how they relate to each other	
Information to help you keep track of your grades for each unit	

Making presentations

Presentations help you to learn communication skills.

Some people hate the idea of standing up to speak in front of an audience. This is quite normal, and you can use the extra energy from nerves to improve your performance.

Presentations aren't some form of torture devised by your tutor! They are included in your course because they help you learn many skills, such as speaking in public and preparing visual aids. They also help you practise working as a team member, and give you a practical reason for researching information. And it can be far more enjoyable to talk about what you've found out rather than write about it!

There's a knack to preparing and giving a presentation so that you use your energies well, don't waste time, don't fall out with everyone around you and keep your stress levels as low as possible. Think about the task in three stages: preparation, organisation and delivery.

Preparation

Start your initial preparations as soon as you can. Putting them off will only cause problems later. Discuss the task in your team so that everyone is clear about what has to be done and how long you have to do it in.

Divide any research fairly among the team, allowing for people's strengths and weaknesses. You'll also need to agree:

- which visual aids would be best
- which handouts you need and who should prepare them
- where and when the presentation will be held, and what you should wear
- what questions you might be asked, both individually and as a team, and how you should prepare for them.

Once you've decided all this, carry out the tasks you've been allocated to the best of your ability and by the deadline agreed.

TOP TIPS

Keep visual aids simple but effective, and check any handouts carefully before you make lots of copies.

Organisation

This is about the planning you need to do as a team so that everything will run smoothly on the day.

Delivery

This refers to your performance during the presentation. Being well prepared and well organised helps you keep calm. If you're very nervous at the start, don't panic – just take a few deep breaths and concentrate on the task, not yourself. It's quite normal to be nervous at the start but this usually fades once you get under way. You might even enjoy it…

Case study: Presenting and sharing work

Presenting and sharing work with other students will be a regular activity on the BTEC First in Media. For example, you might be asked to deliver a PowerPoint presentation about a job role you have researched, or present an animation or video you have created.

The media students at Little Upton High School are undertaking an assignment for Unit 14: Deconstructing Computer Games.

They have been asked to choose a computer game to deconstruct and to present their findings to the rest of the class. They are prepared to be questioned on their presentations and to receive feedback from others in the class.

The fact that they are presenting as individuals, and that they know their work will be discussed by the class and possibly criticised, makes the learners nervous.

Whenever you take part in a session like this, try to put your fellow learners at ease.

If you are watching a presentation:

• remember that criticism should always be constructive – don't simply say you don't like something, try to explain how it could be improved.

• find something good to say about the presentation to balance out any negative comments you might have.

If you are presenting work:

• try not to take criticism personally – it is the work, not you as a person, that is being discussed.

Activity: Preparing, delivering and watching presentations

How well will you cope with the presentations you will have to take part in on your BTEC First? This quiz should get you thinking.

1 You have just finished your presentation deconstructing a computer game. Someone in your class asks a question about an earlier version of the game. You don't know the answer to this question. What do you do?

   a) Try to avoid the question by trying to change the subject

   b) Admit that you don't know the answer

   c) Make something up: the questioner will probably never realise what you have done

2 A student on your course is delivering a presentation and he is obviously very nervous. What do you do?

   a) Sink into your chair with embarrassment

   b) Look at him and smile in an encouraging way

   c) Try to think of a difficult question to ask at the end

3 It is the day before an important presentation and you have forgotten to book a place in the computer suite. This means there is no way you'll get your PowerPoint slides finished in time. What do you do?

   a) Pretend to be unwell

   b) Come clean, apologise, and try to get through the presentation anyway

   c) Blame someone else

4 You have been working as part of a group of four to develop ideas for a short video on road safety. One of your group has not been pulling her weight, and as the presentation approaches you are worried that it will affect the group's performance. What do you do?

   a) Cross your fingers and hope she doesn't turn up for the presentation

   b) Talk to your tutor to get some advice

   c) Lose your temper and tell her not to bother turning up on the day

5 When the time comes to present your group's ideas for the video to the class, you find that the first group to present has come up with a very similar idea to the one your group has chosen. What do you do?

   a) Make an excuse and go to the bathroom when it's your group's turn

   b) Present your idea anyway

   c) Accuse the other group of stealing your idea

Do you think you can improve on the way that you currently cope with presentations?

Your assessments

The importance of assignments

All learners on BTEC First courses are assessed by means of **assignments**. Each one is designed to link to specific **learning outcomes** and **grading criteria**. At the end of the course, your assignment grades put together determine your overall grade.

To get the best grade you can, you need to know the golden rules that apply to all assignments, then how to interpret the specific instructions.

10 golden rules for assignments

1   Check that you understand the instructions.

2   Check whether you have to do all the work on your own, or if you will do some as a member of a group. If you work as a team, you need to identify which parts are your own contributions.

3   Always write down any verbal instructions you are given.

4   Check the final deadline and any penalties for not meeting it.

5   Make sure you know what to do if you have a serious personal problem, eg illness, and need an official extension.

6   Copying someone else's work (**plagiarism**) is a serious offence and is easy for experienced tutors to spot. It's never worth the risk.

7   Schedule enough time for finding out the information and doing initial planning.

8   Allow plenty of time between talking to your tutor about your plans, preparations and drafts, and the final deadline.

9   Don't panic if the assignment seems long or complicated. Break it down into small, manageable chunks.

10   If you suddenly get stuck, ask your tutor to talk things through with you.

Case study: Using feedback effectively

Jason is getting feedback on his first assignment.

'The first assignment for my BTEC Level 2 First in Creative Media Production was completed last week, and ever since I handed it in I have been a bit anxious about how I have done.

'In today's lesson we were each given an assessment feedback sheet for the assignment. It was more detailed than I had expected and really helped me understand how I had done and what I need to do to get a better grade next time.

'The assignment covered grading criteria P2, M2 and D2 of Unit 3: The Creative Media Sector. We had to investigate different job roles in a creative media sector. We had to research the responsibilities of each job role, as well as finding out about the contracts, conditions and typical pay for each of these jobs, and any codes of practice and legal restrictions that apply. I looked at the television and film sector and found out about six different roles, including camera operator and lighting technician. I presented my findings to the class using PowerPoint slides.

'The assessment feedback sheet gives details about what I had done well and has advice about how to improve. My tutor said that I had included enough good detail to achieve a merit, which is what I hoped to achieve. She also said that if i add some more information about the relevant codes of practice and give some more detailed examples, then I could get a distinction for this part of the unit.'

Interpreting the instructions

Most assignments start with a **command word** – describe, explain, evaluate etc. These words relate to how complex the answer should be.

Command words

Learners often don't do their best because they read the command words but don't understand exactly what they have to do. These tables show you what is required for each grade when you see a particular command word.

Command words and obtaining a pass

Complete ...	Complete a form, diagram or drawing.
Demonstrate ...	Show that you can do a particular activity.
Describe ...	Give a clear, straightforward description that includes all the main points.
Identify ...	Give all the basic facts relating to a certain topic.
List ...	Write a list of the main items (not sentences).
Name ...	State the proper terms related to a drawing or diagram.
Outline ...	Give all the main points, but without going into too much detail.
State ...	Point out or list the main features.

Examples:

○ **List** the main features on your mobile phone.

○ **Describe** the best way to greet a customer.

○ **Outline** the procedures you follow to keep your computer system secure.

Command words and obtaining a merit

Analyse ...	Identify the factors that apply, and state how these are linked and how each of them relates to the topic.
Comment on ...	Give your own opinions or views.
Compare ... Contrast ...	Identify the main factors relating to two or more items and point out the similarities and differences.
Competently use ...	Take full account of information and feedback you have obtained to review or improve an activity.
Demonstrate ...	Prove you can carry out a more complex activity.
Describe ...	Give a full description, including details of all the relevant features.
Explain ...	Give logical reasons to support your views.
Justify ...	Give reasons for the points you are making so that the reader knows what you're thinking.
Suggest ...	Give your own ideas or thoughts.

Examples:
- **Explain** why mobile phones are so popular.
- **Describe** the needs of four different types of customers.
- **Suggest** the type of procedures your employer would need to introduce to keep the IT system secure.

Command words and obtaining a distinction

Analyse ...	Identify several relevant factors, show how they are linked, and explain the importance of each.
Compare ... Contrast ...	Identify the main factors in two or more situations, then explain the similarities and differences, and in some cases say which is best and why.
Demonstrate ...	Prove that you can carry out a complex activity, taking into account information you have obtained or received to adapt your original idea.
Describe ...	Give a comprehensive description which tells a story to the reader and shows that you can apply your knowledge and information correctly.
Evaluate ...	Bring together all your information and make a judgement on the importance or success of something.
Explain ...	Provide full details and reasons to support the arguments you are making.
Justify ...	Give full reasons or evidence to support your opinion.
Recommend ...	Weigh up all the evidence to come to a conclusion, with reasons, about what would be best.

Examples:
- **Evaluate** the features and performance of your mobile phone.
- **Analyse** the role of customer service in contributing to an organisation's success.
- **Justify** the main features on the website of a large, successful organisation of your choice.

TRY THIS

Check the command word you are likely to see for each of your units in the **grading grid** in advance. This tells you the **grading criteria** for the unit so that you know the evidence you will have to present.

TOP TIPS

Think of assignments as an opportunity to demonstrate what you've learned and to get useful feedback on your work.

Activity: Being assessed for research tasks

Learners at Little Upton High School are completing an assignment for Unit 3: The Creative Media Sector. The task they are completing requires them to investigate the way in which the creative media sector is structured.

The pass criterion (P1) requires learners to:
- outline the structure of the creative media sector.

The merit criterion (M1) asks them to:
- describe the structure of the creative media sector with some detail and with reference to appropriate illustrative examples.

To achieve the distinction criterion (D1) they must:
- explain the structure of the creative media sector with reference to precise and detailed illustrative examples.

Hannah makes a list of some creative media organisations. For each creative media industry, she provides some brief notes on the general features of organisations in that part of the media.

Naveed provides detailed information about the various creative media industries and gives specific examples of several companies within each industry, comparing them with each other and explaining the differences between these companies in terms of their size, geographic scope and structures. He also observes that companies in some media industries are structured differently from those in other parts of the media. He explains why he thinks this happens.

Lewis describes the different creative media industries and gives examples of some companies within each industry, providing detailed descriptions of their size, geographic scope and structures.

- Who do you think has done enough to achieve a distinction?

- Who would be given a merit?

- Who would be marked at a pass?

Activity: Being assessed for performances and other practical activities

When undertaking research activities, the difference between attaining a pass, merit or a distinction grade is often defined by the specific wording in the grading criteria, such as describe and explain, and can depend on whether you give appropriate and detailed examples. Other means are used to grade work involving performance and practical tasks.

Look at the differences between these groups of phrases which are often found in grading grids. Give examples of what you think you would need to show as evidence to meet the italicised word (or words) in each phrase:

- present an *idea*
- present a *developed* idea
- present an *imaginative* idea

- *apply* techniques
- apply techniques *competently*
- apply techniques *skilfully*

- *partially realises* intentions
- *mainly realises* intentions
- *clearly achieves* intentions

- *review* strengths and weaknesses
- *describe* strengths and weaknesses
- *evaluate* strengths and weaknesses

Sample assignment

Note about assignments
All learners are different and will approach their assignment in different ways.
The sample assignment that follows shows how one learner answered a brief to achieve pass, merit and distinction level criteria. The learner work shows just one way in which grading criteria can be evidenced. There are no standard or set answers. If you produce the required evidence for each task then you will achieve the grading criteria covered by the assignment.

Front sheet

Check the front sheet of your assignment carefully and ensure you complete all necessary fields, eg your name.

Make a note of when the work for the assignment is due and be sure that you know your school or college's policy on meeting deadlines.

Before submitting your work it is useful to run it past your tutor for comment. There may be essential evidence which you have missed.

When putting evidence together, do check that it meets the requirements of the grading criterion. Depending upon the assignment, your evidence could be in the form of written reports, class presentations, audio visual presentations, information you have collected and commented upon, or even a website.

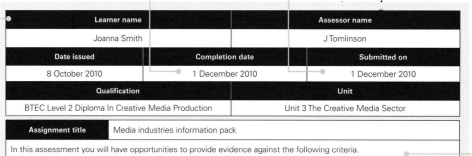

Learner name			Assessor name	
Joanna Smith			J Tomlinson	
Date issued		**Completion date**	**Submitted on**	
8 October 2010		1 December 2010	1 December 2010	
Qualification			**Unit**	
BTEC Level 2 Diploma In Creative Media Production			Unit 3 The Creative Media Sector	

Assignment title	Media industries information pack

In this assessment you will have opportunities to provide evidence against the following criteria. Indicate the page numbers where the evidence can be found.

Criteria reference	To achieve the criteria the evidence must show that the student is able to:	Task no.	Page numbers
P1	outline the structure of the creative media sector		
M1	describe the structure of the creative media sector with some detail and with reference to appropriate illustrative examples	1	3–9
D1	explain the structure of the creative media sector with reference to precise and detailed illustrative examples		
P2	describe job roles and conditions of employment in a creative media industry		
M2	describe job roles and conditions of employment in a creative media industry with some detail and with reference to appropriate illustrative examples	2	9–13
D2	explain job roles and conditions of employment in a creative media industry with reference to precise and detailed illustrative examples		
P3	describe how to obtain employment in a creative media industry		
M3	describe how to obtain employment in a creative media industry with some detail and with reference to appropriate illustrative examples	3	14
D3	explain how to obtain employment in a creative media industry with reference to precise and detailed illustrative examples		
Learner declaration			

I certify that the work submitted for this assignment is my own and research sources are fully acknowledged.

Learner signature: *Joanna Smith*   Date: *1 December 2010*

This grid is very important as it shows how your work will be graded for each of the criteria. Remember also that to achieve a pass, merit or distinction overall, you must achieve at least that grade in all of the criteria.

Make sure that any evidence you present is your own and not copied or cut and pasted from other people's work. If you use quotes from other reference sources, make sure these are clearly referenced.

Assignment brief

Scenarios are intended to help you relate the assignment tasks to the kind of things you may be asked to produce in the media industry, and think about what would be required from you working for a real company or client.

Always keep the assignment title in mind when producing work for your assessment. This will help ensure you produce work appropriate to the topic.

Unit title	Unit 3: The Creative Media Sector
Qualification	BTEC Level 2 Diploma in Creative Media Production
Start date	8 October 2010
Deadline date	1 December 2010
Assessor	J Tomlinson

Assignment title	Media industries information pack

The purpose of this assignment is to:
discuss how the creative media sector is structured, the types of jobs that are available, what those jobs involve, and how they might be obtained.

Scenario
You have been invited by a publishing company to produce an information pack for people who wish to know more about the creative media sector and how to gain employment in it.

The pack is to be distributed to college careers services nationwide. It is to be called: Getting to know the creative media sector. It will need to be lively and engaging, while highlighting and discussing all the relevant points outlined in the tasks.

Task 1
You must start your information pack with a detailed description of the creative media sector. You need to look at each of these media industries:
• television
• radio
• press
• publishing
• film
• interactive media
• computer games
• photography and photo imaging
• advertising and marketing.

Describe the characteristics of typical businesses in each of these media industries, including their geographical scope (for example, multinational, national, local), status (for example, small-size and medium-size businesses, independent, subsidiary), structure (for example, private, public, cross-media). Include a range of illustrative examples of companies that operate in each of these industries.

This provides evidence for P1, M1 and D1

Task 2
In the next section, you need to describe and explain job roles within a creative media industry:

Provide the reader with information about possible jobs roles that are available in one of the industries listed in Task 1 and provide some detailed illustrative examples of specific jobs.

In addition, provide the reader with an idea of the working conditions within the industry you have chosen, considering issues such as professional codes of practice and conduct, hours, salary and typical contracts of employment.

This provides evidence for P2, M2 and D2

Professional practice refers to the codes of practice in the industry (eg advertising standards) and legal restrictions (eg libel law) with which workers may have to comply.

Name and discuss companies which are well known or which are good examples of the type of company in each sector.

Personal attributes might include your punctuality, reliability and self-presentation, communication and teamwork skills.

Task 3

In the final section give your readers advice on the routes available to them which can help them gain employment in a creative media industry:

Revisit the industry you selected for Task 2, and outline and explain the possible routes to gaining employment in this industry, such as education and voluntary work. Detail the skills and attributes that will be most beneficial to working in this industry – these can include technical and creative skills, as well as personal attributes.

You must also include advice about where to look for jobs within this creative media industry, providing examples.

This provides evidence for P3, M3 and D3

Final assignment evidence

A completed 'media guide' in your chosen format for example:
• a PowerPoint presentation
• a leaflet or booklet.

Include references to the information sources you consulted in your research.

Sources of information

Baylis, P. and Procter, N. – *BTEC First Creative and Media* (Pearson, 2010)
Branston, G. and Stafford, R. – *The Media Student's Book*, fourth edition (Routledge, 2006)
O'Sullivan, T., Dutton, B. and Rayner, P. – *Studying the Media: An Introduction* (Arnold, 2003)

Websites

www.bbc.co.uk – The BBC website
www.bbfc.co.uk – The British Board of Film Classification
www.bfi.org.uk – The British Film Institute
www.carlton.com – Carlton TV
www.channel4.com – Channel 4 TV
www.granada.co.uk – Granada TV
www.guardianjobs.co.uk – A good site for exploring media jobs, see also *The Guardian* on Mondays
www.mediaknowall.com – A good starting point for internet research on the media
www.mediaweek.co.uk – Media news, comment and blogs
www.newscorp.com – News Corporation
www.ofcom.org.uk – The independent regulator for the UK communications industries
www.radiocentre.org – Organisation representing UK commercial radio stations

This brief has been verified as being fit for purpose			
Assessor	J Tomlinson		
Signature	J Tomlinson	Date	1 September 2010
Internal verifier	K Harris		
Signature	K Harris	Date	1 September 2010

The sources of information are included to give you some good places to start looking for the information you need to collect.

Sample learner work

BTEC FIRST DIPLOMA CREATIVE MEDIA PRODUCTION

Getting to know the creative media sector

Creating an index for your submission means that the assessor can quickly get an overview of what is covered in your work.

Sample learner work

| Page 2 | GETTING TO KNOW THE CREATIVE MEDIA SECTOR |

INDEX

It is a good idea to split your work down into clear sub-headings that address each area of the brief.

The learner starts well by naming some of the companies within the industry and talking a little about the geographical scope, but not in much detail.

Sample learner work

Page 3 — GETTING TO KNOW THE CREATIVE MEDIA SECTOR

1. Media Industries

The media industries have a huge impact in our daily lives; something that used to be a very small industry two centuries ago has now become the largest communication system in the world. It started with printing followed by the radio and ended up with several huge and successful industries. Let's have a look at the different industries in the media.

1.1 Television

The television has been providing us with entertainment and news since the thirties. The TV industry produces either recorded material (DVD's) or broadcast material. The latter, however, is most frequently watched.

There are two types of channels; the first type of channel is terrestrial, these are local/national channels. BBC1, BB2, ITV, Channel4 and Five are UK based terrestrial channels and can be watched without any TV satellite provider. Secondly there are satellite channels, channels from all over the world. In order to watch these you need to have a contract with a satellite channel provider such as BSkyB[1] and Virgin Media in Britain.

The Television industry produces several entertaining, informative and educational programmes categorized in different genres. Those genres include sitcoms, comedies, talk shows, drama, news and current affairs, reality shows, cartoons, and lots more. The genre of programmes that are broadcasted depends on what channel you're watching. For example if you are watching a music channel it will only broadcast programmes that are somehow related to music. And what about those short ads in between the programmes? Television is a very useful medium for advertisers, which is why they sponsor several channels to let their commercials broadcast. Whether a channel can air an advertisement depends on what type of channel it is. If it is totally funded by the government (the licence fee from everyone who owns a TV set), it is not allowed to show any adverts. In order to watch television programmes you are required to be covered by a valid TV Licence. No matter what medium you are using; computer, mobile phone, DVD recorder, etc. as long as the programmes you watch are being broadcast on the TV, you will always be asked to have a licence. If you're using any device that is only used for production of sounds and is not used to watch TV programmes, you don't need to pay a licence fee.

In the UK, the BBC is a Public Service Broadcaster and runs its UK based channels through the budget that it gets from the government. Other broadcasters rely on advertisers, sponsors and programme sales to be able to run their channels.

Television broadcasters in the United Kingdom are regulated by the Office of Communication, also known as OfCom. OfCom makes sure that the consumers are satisfied with services they get from their providers. The organization manages to do that through

[1] British Sky Broadcasting

The learner includes a lot of information here, but much of it is not related to the points required by the brief or the unit content.

Footnotes can be used to explain abbreviations used in the text, or to expand on what you are saying.

This information is relevant to the structure of the companies (public/privately owned) but this could be expressed more directly, eg 'other broadcasters are privately owned and…'

Look back over the last section. Has the learner talked about the status (eg size) of the businesses as required by the brief?

This information is relevant to the structure of the companies (public/privately owned) but this could be expressed more directly, eg 'commercial broadcasters are privately owned and…'

Sample learner work

| Page 4 | GETTING TO KNOW THE CREATIVE MEDIA SECTOR |

consulting people, asking for their views about certain topics and by letting them complain if they feel that the content is unsuitable or offensive.

1.2 Radio

The radio industry includes all the services that provide radio programming. Radio broadcasts are entirely audio based and are transmitted to the public through radio waves. This industry is responsible for production of different programmes such as music programmes, news-updates, talk shows, comedy programmes, sports coverage, lifestyle programmes and much more. Enjoying this programming in Britain is possible on terrestrial radio channels[2] and satellite radio channels.

There are two kinds of radio broadcasters. Firstly, Public Service Broadcasters, they are financed totally or partly through license fee by the government. The second type is the Independent Local Radio is also known as, Commercial Broadcasters. They are financed through sales of adverts on their channel. The advertisers pay for advertising space on their radio channel.

There are different kinds of radio stations; starting with the commercial AM – FM radio. Also known as terrestrial radio, it is the most common and the most used among all. It has a huge number of listeners, including drivers, whom it provides with a lot of entertainment, news and traffic-updates and informative programmes.

In the second place there is Satellite Radio; to be able to listen to a satellite radio channel you need to pay a monthly subscription, you can have good quality radio coverage and a much wider range of channels of all genres.

Last but not least, the Internet Radio, that took off in the early nineties. This phenomenon made listening to radio much easier than it was before and provides a wider range of radio channels than satellite radio does. You can listen to any radio channel from any place through radio streaming.

Like TV channels, Radio broadcasting is regulated by OfCom. They are meant to deal with consumers' complaints, making codes of conduct and dealing with other matters to ensure the consumers' comfort.

---

[2](BBC Radio 1, BBC 1Xtra, BBC Radio 2,BBC Radio 3, BBC Radio 4, BBC Radio Five Live, BBC Five Live Sports Extra, BBC 6 Music, BBC 7, BBC Asian Network, BBC World Service, The Hits Radio, Smash Hits!, Kiss, Heat, Magic, Q, 102.2 Smooth Radio, BBC Radio Scotland, BBC Radio nan Gaidheal, BBC Radio Foyle, Kerrang!, talkSPORT, 3C, Premier Christian Radio, U105, Absolute Radio, Heart 106.2)

The learner mentions codes of conduct which are relevant to criterion 2, but not to criterion 1 which is being assessed by this task.

Review what is asked for by the brief. Is there any additional information you think the learner could have included in this section?

The learner has given a historical overview but has not named any companies, or talked about them is terms of status, geographical scope, structure etc.

The learner names some job roles which are relevant to criterion 2, but not to criterion 1 which is being assessed by this task.

Sample learner work

Page 5	GETTING TO KNOW THE CREATIVE MEDIA SECTOR

1.3 Press

Press is one of the most ancient types of media in the world; it started in the 15th century and still goes on. It's a way of providing any kind of text based information to the reader. The information depends on what type and genre of printed item you're reading. These different types of published items vary from magazines, broadsheets to tabloids and gossip. Some of them are globally renowned which is why they are available in every single corner of the world.

Publishing started on a really small scale. The main reason behind publishing leaflets and newspapers was to update people about the politics and everything that was going on in their region. It was also a way to express their opinion or criticize the government. Because there was only a small number of educated citizens, this phenomenon wasn't accessible for everybody but for those who could afford education. The readers of newspapers and other published articles belonged mostly to high society circles and the bourgeoisie.

There is now a wider range of published items, such as: books, magazines, newspapers, leaflets, scripts, etc. All of these are classified by genre. The genres vary from music, gaming, lifestyle, fashion to gardening and a lot more. And again, this medium serves for advertising. Advertisers use leaflets, page spreads in magazines and newspapers to promote their products.

The press staff consists of editors, journalists, writers, photographers, and loads more people in this industry put a lot of work into the kind of product they are publishing. Just imagine the daily broadsheets we get in our mailbox, the 20 page broadsheet is NOT fallen from the sky, it is done by people who are part of the press industry.

1.4 Publishing

Publishing is very closely linked to the press as it is the process by which Newspapers and Magazines are printed, marketed and distributed, however there as also many other sides to publishing, especially in this modern day and age. Publishing will include more traditional formats such as books but will now also deal with products such as e-books, websites and other electronic media, as well as musical works and software. Much of this work will have what id known as a copyright on it which is shows that it is an original work and someone's intellectual property. Copyright is very important as it allows authors etc, full rights over their own work and ensures that they receive the full payment for them rather than having someone else rip them off and make money off of their idea.

The learner mentions copyright, which may be relevant to professional working practices in criterion 2, but not to criterion 1 which is being assessed by this task.

The learner names some companies and identifies them as being large, but isn't very specific about what the statement means, eg national/multinational, large annual sales, owning several smaller companies?

This information is good, but would have been better if the learner had specified which companies were being referred to rather than saying 'Many publishing companies ...'.

Sample learner work

| Page 6 | GETTING TO KNOW THE CREATIVE MEDIA SECTOR |

Publishing has many stages and each stage had specialised jobs and roles to be carried out. The process begins with concept and design and finished with the actual printing so there are a range of Creative and Technical jobs such as Writing and Graphic Design, Editing and Printing and even Proof-reading; all of these jobs are important to the entire process and have their own specialised skills.

There are many large scale Publishing Companies, familiar ones you may have heard of are Penguin Books, which are often know for publishing children's books as well as classics and handbooks which were practical guides on a number of different topics such as cookery or even legal advice. Some companies, such a Pearson will specialise in academic publishing, which is books and materials sold to schools, colleges and universities, these are aiming at providing information and aiding study, they are usually factual and cover a specific subject area such as Biology, History, and Mathematics etc.

Many publishing companies are a media conglomerate, which means they are an amalgamation of many different smaller companies that have merged together and that have interests in lots of different media productions such as publishing, Television, radio etc. They will usually be based in one country, such as London in the UK for example but also have branches and companies all over the world, this means that they can work in loads of different markets at the same time.

1.5 Film

From silent to classical and now to the modern era, the film industry has evolved dramatically within the last century. It has grown to the largest money making industry in the world. It involves a number of production companies, movie studios, festivals, award shows, etc. Countless **directors, producers, actors, scriptwriters, camera crews, set designers** and other film staff find their way in the listed branches.

Production companies are very important in this industry. They were founded in order to make film production easier and affordable by providing film makers less expensive equipment. A few examples of world renowned production companies are *20 Century Fox, Warner Bros, Sony Pictures* and *the Walt Disney Company*

In the UK films (along with video games) are regulated by BBFC (British Board of Film Classification). It's a non-governmental organization that was founded to focus on film and video game classification.

The most recognized film industries can be found in the United Stated, India, Hong Kong and Nigeria. The American film industry is older than any other film industry in the world. Since

The learner names some job roles which are relevant to criterion 2, but not to criterion 1 which is being assessed by this task.

This information may be relevant to professional working practices in criterion 2, but not to criterion 1 which is being assessed by this task.

Review what is asked for by the brief. Is there any additional information you think the learner could have included in this section?

The italics and speech marks help show this is a quotation, and the number relates to the footnote which shows where the quotation is taken from. It is important to make sure that any quotations used show their source.

Sample learner work

| Page 7 | **GETTING TO KNOW THE CREATIVE MEDIA SECTOR** |

production companies were largely concentrated in California, the word "Hollywood" has come to mean (connotational meaning) "the American film industry". However, Hollywood has managed to release some of the biggest blockbusters known everywhere across the world (*e.g.: Titanic*). It has introduced legends like Marilyn Monroe and John Wayne.

The industry produces many film genres including comedy, romance, thrillers, horrors, animation films, science/pulp fiction, documentary's. All of them are made in movie studios on different ways with different effects. The success booked by the film depends on the amount of sold tickets and Oscar nominations.

1.6 Interactive Media

"Interactive media is the integration of digital media including combinations of electronic text, graphics, moving images, and sound, into a structured digital computerized environment that allows people to interact with the data for appropriate purposes. The digital environment can include the Internet, telecoms and interactive digital television."[3]

In other words, Interactive media is the kind of media that allows us to interact with each other using all kinds of digital media applications through communication services like the internet. It is in fact any form of multimedia technology that is capable of creating dialogue between the consumers of it.

It is a part of the media that is capable of getting involved in every single facet of our lives. It educates us, keeps us updated and makes all our activities easier. More specifically, all you need to do is add an 'E' (which stands for electronic) and there it goes! Activities like booking flights, shopping, banking, etc. are now available online. Remarkable is that all these agencies, organisations and companies are highly advising their clients to use online services. They motivate their clients by making online services cheaper through promotions and other ways of thanking their customers for having used the e-services.

Other than that, the main reason behind Interactive Media is to make the world a smaller place, a village as globalists intend to name it. It doesn't matter where you are, what you're doing, just a single click with your mouse can make you closer to the rest of the world.

1.7 Computer Games

Computer and video games, the ultimate entertainment source of this new era; the gaming industry has developed amazingly over the last ten years. Who would have thought they would experience the launch of Play Station 3, when they were just getting used to the first version? Who thought Nitendo would ever bring Nintendo DS "portable" and Wii into the market? Who would possibly have thought they could go gaming in 3D in the cinema's instead of watching a movie? The same goes for Microsoft's Xbox 360 and several computer

---

[3] Definition, Interactive Media – Source: http://www.atsf.co.uk/atsf/interactive_media.pdf

The learner hasn't named any specific companies. Is there any additional information you think the learner should have included in this section?

The learner has talked about specific companies, but has not included information about their size, shape and structure.

Be careful to proofread your work as well as just using a computer spellchecker, which may not pick up if company or product names have been spelled incorrectly.

Sample learner work

Page 8 | GETTING TO KNOW THE CREATIVE MEDIA SECTOR

games. The development of technology has a had a great influence on the interactive side of the media, the consoles and computer games kept getting better and better, and ended up with a bigger target audience than ever before. Remember when gaming was only referred to nerds and young boys! Well, that's not the case anymore! Companies have issued different themes along with their new consoles, so that people can choose for CD-ROMs or theme based memory cards that appeal to them. Take "Guitar Hero" for instance, this was specially aimed for rock music enthusiasts, it has spinoffs for computers, Mac's, Nitendo DS and – Lite.

The rising popularity of video/computer gaming wasn't undiscovered by companies in other media sectors. Major record labels and film producers found ways to make more money out of it. Record labels got a second chance to issue games featuring the stars they were representing, e.g.: Hannah Montana, Aerosmith. Not only record labels were the ones to see this opportunity, even sports enthusiast found faces of their idols on game discs, e.g.: Tony Hawks, David Beckham, Cristiano Ronaldo, Roger Federer, Rafael Nadal, etc. Another example from the movies is Harry Potter, its success didn't stop the producers to launch more gadgets with his face on since he was the sensation of that particular moment.

To conclude, it is pretty clear that the gaming industry is one of the biggest among interactive media. The growing technology and features in the consoles has the power to attract any kind of audience by targeting their weaknesses for certain personalities, music genre or movies. The spacing between young and old, new and old generation is filling up as it seems.

1.8 Photography and photo imaging

Photo imaging is not only used in media industries but in any other industry you can think of. It has always been considered as the hidden industry yet a very important one. A lot of organization, work and effort are put into making relevant pictures that can possibly be published.

The process starts with just like in any other media industry with brainstorming about what the client wants photographed; who is it meant for and what are the main purposes behind the production. Followed by sorting out the location and (if needed) finding a model. The actual work begins after having worked on all the above and it doesn't stop after having a couple of good shots. That's where it actually begins; a lot of digital editing needs to be done afterwards to make it look like the client want it to be (post-production).

A picture needs to be different, persuasive, and extraordinarily attractive. Advertisers often intend to spend a lot of money on celebs; this is another strategy to make people buy a certain product. For instance, how many people wouldn't have bought this Givenchy fragrance after

The learner names some job roles which are relevant to criterion 2, but not to criterion 1 which is being assessed by this task.

Review what is asked for by the brief. Is there any additional information you think the learner should have included in this section?

Sample learner work

Page 9	GETTING TO KNOW THE CREATIVE MEDIA SECTOR

seeing Justin Timberlake posing with it? – How many party people wouldn't have added Martini to their drinks when George Clooney said: "No Martini, no party!"

In the media, photo imaging is used to promote new artists, bands, and new media. Also, photography is a very important part in the fashion industry. **Photographers** are behind those extraordinary pictures of models (who get the most of the credit). Magazines are used to publish those pictures often to promote **fashion designers.**

1.9 Advertising and Marketing

Marketing and advertising is a very powerful industry to promote any product. It is an individual industry to which a lot of other industries are dependant. It manipulates, advises and persuades people to buy a certain product, which is why it is used everywhere. Media industries are either a medium for advertising or they can be clients of marketers.

A lot of different strategies are used to make products sell. We, the modern society, are manipulated continuously, conscious and unconsciously. Advertisers and marketers know how to target us. Ever wondered why IKEA makes us walk through the whole complex before we can get our hands on what we actually came to look for? Or why your favourite celebrity appears in advertisements promoting a drink you have never tried before?

This branch of the media is not only used to make products sell but also to promote new artists, bands, announcing tours, festivals and concerts.

2. Let's have a detailed look at the Television Industry...

2.1 Job roles and recruitment

This section describes different job roles in the television industry: here the workforce consists of various job roles such as journalism, radio and TV presenting. Some job roles are independent, but if one wants to have a stable and bright career, it is advisable to find a post in a broadcasting company. People working within a broadcasting company vary from directors, producers; camera operators, presenters, sound technicians, editors, costume and properties designers, researchers and runners etc... 3 of them are described in detail below.

To enter the broadcasting world professionally, several companies would expect you to demonstrate and have a huge interest in television production as well as being a consumer of this media. Note that you can't make it into this creative industry if you don't know

The title clearly shows which industry the learner is looking at in more detail.

The learner starts by listing a range of different jobs, and will then go on to talk about some of them in more detail.

What grade do you think the learner will have been given for this task and why? What feedback would you give to the learner? On page 62 you can see the grades and feedback that the assessor has given.

The different types of contract are described in some detail, eg describing that freelance workers will not get sick pay. This means the learner is working towards merit level for criterion 2.

Sample learner work

| Page 10 | GETTING TO KNOW THE CREATIVE MEDIA SECTOR |

anything about it. It is necessary for an applicant to have knowledge about it to a certain extent. A degree in that particular field is the best way to show that you have what it takes.

You may be recruited under different contracts such as freelance/fixed-term, full-time (permanent), part-time (permanent), shift work, office hours, irregular, salaried, voluntary work, internship or on completion. The kind of contract you get from the employer depends on what you're specialized in, to what extent the label needs your support in the project or the level of reliability you show them. You can also go for self-employment, depending on what you actually are aiming for. Here are some examples of contracts you might be offered and what they involve:

Freelance & Fixed-term

Freelance contracts don't require work on a permanent basis; they are meant to last for a certain period of time (often 1 year). The only difference between a freelance and a fixed-term contract is that the latter is still somehow linked to the company even if the contract gets expired. While freelance, breaks any kind of connection with the employer after the expiration of the contract. Freelance workers are also responsible for paying their own tax and will not get sick pay, holiday pay or other benefits.

Voluntary work

Voluntary based contracts work on the idea of working without salary. People are interested in this kind of work to gain experience, to be helpful and fill their CV's with positive references that might help them getting well-paid jobs in the future. The concept of this type of contract might be hard to understand but working voluntarily undoubtedly has its own advantages.

Full-time (permanent)

Full-time contracts are the most common ones among all of the listed contracts. This contract makes you an official member of the team and you can get several benefits like pension, sick pay, maternity/paternity and holiday pay. In order to fulfil all requirements of this contract you have work full time which is usually 30 – 40 hours a week.

For each job role the learner gives examples of what the role might entail, which provides evidence towards merit level for criteria 2. However, more precise and detailed descriptions would be needed to attain distinction level.

The learner includes a great list of skills that might be required of a producer, and it's a really good idea put the important word in bold to highlight them. Unfortunately this information is relevant to criterion 3, not criterion 2 which is being assessed by this task, so it might be missed by the assessor.

Sample learner work

Page 11   **GETTING TO KNOW THE CREATIVE MEDIA SECTOR**

2.1.1   Career profiles

TELEVISION PRODUCER

Producers are very important for all broadcasting companies; in fact they are the ones that organise production from start to finish. They guide, plan and coordinate the production team throughout the rehearsals and filming process, they also ensure that funding is in place and is used effectively. After this process they also oversee editors and other post-production personnel to bring the product together on schedule and on budget. Once a product is completed it is all about marketing and distribution, since producers are key personnel behind the whole production process they will also need to have a good knowledge and understanding of the entire process and have a good idea of how and when the product will be released onto the market, they will also of had to ensure that the funding had been put in place for this before production began.

RECRUITMENT

<u>SKILLS:</u> The broadcast industry requires **educated and experienced** producers with a sound sense and understanding of the entire production process. Producers lead the whole process; therefore they need good **persuasion and leadership skills**. Since they need to assist in the recruitment process for technical and creative staff, they need to have an **eye for talent** and **good judgment skills**. Producers are also behind the securing of funding for the project so being able to **understand budgets and** work within them is a very important point and having a **good business/marketing sense** would be very helpful in this case. A lot of work is put into the editing process which requires a lot of **patience** as well as **technical skills, a producer will need to be able to work along side the director and other creative and technical staff in this area and ensure that the project is completed on schedule whilst not compromising the overall quality of the final product**. Last but not least, to be able to work in a group, spending a lot of hours in a team and get a project done within limited time needs good **communication skills** and the **ability to work under pressure**.

<u>QUALIFICATIONS:</u> for this job role, being passionate is as valuable as any qualification. Still, it is also necessary to have some technical skills, you can gain these through many different courses as well as on the job training, a couple of university and college courses are listed below.

- BA (Honors) Media Production (Provided by several universities in the UK)
- BTEC Higher National Diploma Media Production (College course)
- BTEC National Diploma Media Production (Television and Film)

The learner writes about the types of guidelines that a producer would have to adhere to and gives a good example which will help to achieve a merit in this criterion.

For each job role the learner gives examples of what the role might entail, which provides evidence towards merit level for criterion 2. However, more precise and detailed descriptions would be needed to attain distinction level.

The learner includes a great list of skills that might be required, but this information is relevant to criterion 3, not criterion 2 which is being assessed by this task, so it might be missed by the assessor.

Sample learner work

Page 12	GETTING TO KNOW THE CREATIVE MEDIA SECTOR

PROFESSIONAL WORKING PRACTICES: A producer will have to make sure that they and their staff stick within the law and within the guidelines set down by the company they are working for. For instance if they are producing for the BBC, they must stick to the BBC Guidelines which say that the information in programmes must be accuarate, impartial and fair. This is the same whether producing for TV or Radio. For example, in 2008 when Russell Brand and Jonathan Ross made prank phone calls on Radio 2 they were accused of breaching BBC guidelines on taste and decency and the producer had to apologise for allowing it to happen.

EDITOR

The Editors role is during the Post-Production phase, they make the masses of footage and the Directors vision come alive. Footage will have been shot out of sequence according to when and where filming took place so the Editor has to put all of this in the right order. Sometimes they need to suggest ideas when what they are asked for either won't work or could be improved, there is collaboration involved as well as individual work so Editors don't always spend hours on end on their own. With today's programme content there is a lot more involved than just adding transitions and title sequences, or adding and syncing music, very often programmes will contain Special Effects (SFX) to make things happen or appear that weren't there in the first place. This is a very specialised skill and requires painstaking patience and attention to detail, as well as a high level technical competence with the latest Editing hardware and Software.

RECRUITMENT

SKILLS: First of all to get a post as an Editor it is obvious that you have **to be familiar with the software programs**, you also need experience of working with the hardware too. The more programmes you are familiar and competent with the more versatile you will seem to an employer; however you will need to keep up to date with industry standards at all times. As you will be using creative vision as well as technical skills having a degree that proves that you have the basic skills and vision would be helpful, on the job training is also invaluable so be prepared to work for free or very little while you learn the ropes, there are also intensive short courses available. You will also need good communication and interpersonal skills as you will often be working as part of a team and will have to interpret the ideas of others and bring them to life.

The learner writes about the types of guidelines that an editor would have to adhere to, but could include more detail and examples.

For each job role the learner gives examples of what the role might entail, which provides evidence towards merit level for criterion 2. However, more precise and detailed descriptions would be needed to attain distinction level.

The learner talks about entering the industry via internship, which doesn't really fit under the 'Skills' heading but would be great information to add to the 'Finding a job' section on the next page.

Sample learner work

Page 13	GETTING TO KNOW THE CREATIVE MEDIA SECTOR

QUALIFICATIONS:

- BTEC Higher/National Diploma in Media/Interactive Media (Available in colleges)
- BA (hons) Visual Effects and Animation (Available in specialist Universities)
- 3 Week Editing Course (Met Film School)

PROFESSIONAL WORKING PRACTICES: An editor will normally work with a producer and will have to work under the same guidelines. They might also have to worry about copyright if they are editing together pieces of footage from other sources.

MUSIC JOURNALIST

Music journalists write about music and everything that includes music business. Music journalism covers different kinds writing; some journalists are strictly specialised in reviewing, other ones would rather write about artists and interview them and some others concentrate on the on the music business on its own and whatever catches the readers interest in this field. Publications appear in different magazines and newspapers; but it depends to what extent the magazine or newspaper cover music related articles. There are a lot of advantages of working as a music journalist. Since you have to review music, you get to hear pre-released tracks. Secondly, you get the opportunity to see your favourite music personalities, and count in that you will most probably be invited in after parties and get free passes for several events. Having advantages means there are also disadvantages in the field; a lot effort is needed in this field since you have to work independently and you will certainly be dealing with deadlines.

RECRUITMENT

SKILLS: A lot of people believe that the best way of breaking into this industry is through **internships** because there's always a chance that they may turn into real job opportunities. Being a music journalist requires the ability of **working under pressure**, since you will have get pieces done within a limited period of time. If you work in an editorial team, be ready to get projects on topics (or musicians in this case) you haven't heard about before, a lot of **research** and **patience** will be needed here. If you are asked to work in team on a project, having good **communication skills** is another requirement.

The learner writes about the types of guidelines that a journalist would have to adhere to and gives a good example which will help to achieve a merit in this criteria.

It would be clearer for the assessor if the numbering related to the tasks, so this became Section 3 (as it relates to Task 3) rather than Section 2.1.2.

Sample learner work

| Page 14 | GETTING TO KNOW THE CREATIVE MEDIA SECTOR |

QUALIFICATIONS:

- BTEC Higher/National Diploma in Media (College course)
- Media and Communication (University level)
- Creative writing and journalism (University level)
- Media Studies (University level)
- Journalism (University level)
- Creative Studies and Music (University level)

PROFESSIONAL WORKING PRACTICES: As well as working within the company guidelines like those of the BBC, all journalists have to be especially careful to work within press codes of conduct. The National Union of Journalists has a code to make sure it's members maintain the highest professional and ethical standards. They also need to make sure not to break libel law. Libel is you say someone in writing which is untrue and could damage their reputation.

2.1.2 Finding a job

The previous section explains everything about the jobs in the television industry and on what basis people are recruited. The following and final part of this guide is all about how to find a job in the television industry and where to look for it. There are different sources you can use to find a job, local and national press are some of the most common sources. That's the first choice that comes into people's mind when they are in this position.

Another option is the internet, there are a number of interim websites where you can fill in your details and submit your CV, and they forward your details to several interested employers. Note that, your CV needs to be attractive (as in: work experience, availability, etc.) because it's on that basis employers will decide whether or not you are the right person to get the job.

Websites, such as BBC have a 'Careers' webpage specially dedicated to people who want to make a career in the media. It provides details such as: what kind of jobs is available? How many branches (on different places in the country) there are? What kind of people is immediately needed in those branches? What qualities they need to have? There is also an option to submit your CV and details if you are interested. Sometimes companies leave out the 'SUBMIT YOUR CV' part, and add a question sheet instead. This is because they might not have enough time to go through all the CV's they get posted and want to avoid extra information. Depending on the information you provide they will decide if they will contact you through the telephone or even ask you to visit them for an interview (that's where you can present your CV if you haven't done it online).

Congratulations! You're now a member of our team!

The learner provides a simple list of starting points but doesn't go into sufficient detail about how to obtain employment in the creative media industry. Qualifications and transferable skills should be shown in this section too.

A bibliography is a list of all the books and publications you have used. It is important to show where you have researched all information in this way. The learner could have also used this to show that they had looked at magazines, newspapers etc.

Sample learner work

Page 15   GETTING TO KNOW THE CREATIVE MEDIA SECTOR

3 Bibliography

WEBSITE URL's:

en.wikipedia.org
www.ofcom.org.uk
www.tvlicensing.co.uk/aboutus/index.jsp
www.atsf.co.uk/atsf/interactive_media.pdf
weblogs.nrc.nl/wereld/2009/03/01/filmindustrie-profiteert-van-recessie/
www.publications.parliament.uk/pa/cm200203/cmselect/cmcumeds/
667/667.pdf
www.guidance-research.org/future-trends/media/info/trends/photo
www.cvtips.com/employment/jobs_in_television.html
www.sonymusic.co.uk/texts/jobs/
www.schoolsintheusa.com/careerprofiles_details.cfm?CarID=1029
www.accesstomusic.co.uk/courses/further_courses/apprenticeships/
documents/FMA09.pdf
www.ucas.ac.uk
www.skillset.com

Assessor's comments

The Y/N (Yes/No) shows whether each of the criteria has been achieved. For any assignment always check that you are achieving at least all the pass (P) criteria. To achieve an overall pass for a unit you must get all the Ps signed off. Miss out on just one of them and the unit could be lost.

Qualification	BTEC Level 2 Diploma in Creative Media Production	Year	2010–2011
Unit number and title	Unit 3: The Creative Media Sector	Learner name	Joanna Smith

Grading criteria	Achieved?
P1 outline the structure of the creative media sector	N
P2 describe job roles and conditions of employment in a creative media industry	Y
P3 describe how to obtain employment in a creative media industry	N
M1 describe the structure of the creative media sector with some detail and with reference to appropriate illustrative examples	N
M2 describe job roles and conditions of employment in a creative media industry with some detail and with reference to appropriate illustrative examples	Y
M3 describe how to obtain employment in a creative media industry with some detail and with reference to appropriate illustrative examples	N
D1 explain the structure of the creative media sector with reference to precise and detailed illustrative examples	N
D2 explain job roles and conditions of employment in a creative media industry with reference to precise and detailed illustrative examples	N
D3 explain how to obtain employment in a creative media industry with reference to precise and detailed illustrative examples	N

Learner feedback

I am disappointed with my grade and would like to improve it. I am going to make corrections to my pack and resubmit.

Assessor feedback

Your guide is well written and well structured.

Task 1:
You will need to look again at the task to make sure that you fully understand what it is asking for. You have concentrated on issues such as TV show genres, types of radio station, the history of the printed word, but you have not provided evidence of understanding the structure of the media industries as requested. Think about the dominant characteristics in each media industry, such as its geographical reach, and the size and structure of businesses that operate in the industry. Identify some companies that have these characteristics.

Task 2:
You have focused on some specific job roles in the television industry and have shown an understanding of contracts of employment in this section of your guide – well done. You have provided illustrative examples that highlight the skills and qualifications required to gain employment in this industry. To improve, you will need to give more detail, including an explanation of the main jobs in the television industry (full coverage is required), information about how these relate to one another, and more precise examples relating to professional working practice.

Task 3:
Your final section describes places that people can look when searching for a job in the television industry. However, there is not sufficient detail to cover the requirements for P3, M3 or D3. Think about other places where people can find out about job vacancies in the industry, and give some named examples. Explain the process of obtaining employment in television. It could be useful to give some case studies of people who now have job roles in the industry – explaining how they went about seeking work and describing what they did up to the time that they were appointed in the job role. You have included some good detailed information about the skills and attributes required for each job role you have written about in Task 2 but this information needs to be moved to relate to what is required in Task 3.

You should always read and take note of the assessor's feedback; in this case they have praised the learner. Detailing what you enjoyed and also any problems that you had will help you in future assignments. It may also help your tutor when they come to revise the assignment, and this could help future learners.

It is important to give the assessor some feedback here. If you don't understand what you need to do to improve, say so! If you intend to improve your work, this is where you agree it with the assessor and make it clear you know what criteria you need to improve

The action plan should list exactly what you need to do to improve your grade.

Action plan			
Review the first and final sections of your guide.			
Revisit the task instructions and think about what we have covered in this unit so far and how additional information could be included.			
Assessor signature	J Tomlinson	**Date**	17 December 20.10
Learner signature	Joanne Smith	**Date**	21 December 2010

Coping with problems

Most learners sail through their BTEC First with no major problems. Unfortunately, not everyone is so lucky. Some may have personal difficulties or other issues that disrupt their work so they are late handing in their assignments. If this happens to you, it's vital to know what to do. This checklist should help.

Checklist for coping with problems

✔ Check that you know who to talk to.

✔ Don't sit on a problem and worry about it. Talk to someone promptly, in confidence. It's always easier to cope if you've shared it with someone.

✔ Most centres have professional counsellors you can talk to if you prefer. They won't repeat anything you say to them without your permission.

✔ If you've done something wrong or silly, people will respect you more if you are honest, admit where you went wrong and apologise promptly.

Case study: Dealing with problems

Mahmuda has lots of personal problems. Her grandmother in India is very ill and her mother has gone to look after her. Mahmuda's father works long hours at the local factory, leaving Mahmuda to look after her three younger brothers. She is responsible for feeding the family, washing and ironing their clothes, and getting the boys to school.

Mahmuda finds this very difficult as she is currently in the middle of her BTEC First in Creative Media Production course and has lots of assignments to complete and the deadlines are getting nearer. She hasn't told anyone about her situation but feels that she can't cope any longer.

Mahmuda starts to fall behind with her assignments and fails to hand in two on time. Unaware of her situation, Mahmuda's tutor tells her off for missing the deadlines and decides to discipline her, which could lead to temporary exclusion or being asked to leave the course altogether. Mahmuda bursts into tears and the tutor takes her into a quiet room to talk. Mahmuda tells her everything, but doesn't want anyone else to know.

The tutor wishes Mahmuda had spoken to her earlier and suggests that she should make an appointment with the student counselling staff. Mahmuda does this and is surprised to find how much help is available. Mahmuda's councillor arranges extensions on her assignments until her mother returns from India and some one-to-one help at support workshops.

What would you do if you had a problem like Mahmuda? What could Mahmuda have done differently to help herself?

Skills building

To do your best in your assignments you need a number of skills, including:

- your **personal, learning and thinking skills**
- your **functional skills** of ICT, mathematics and English
- your proofreading and document-production skills.

Personal, learning and thinking skills (PLTS)

These are the skills, personal qualities and behaviour that you find in people who are effective and confident at work. These people enjoy carrying out a wide range of tasks, always try to do their best, and work well alone or with others. They enjoy a challenge and use new experiences to learn and develop.

Activity: How good are your PLTS?

1 Do this quiz to help you identify areas for improvement.

a) I get on well with other people.

Always   **Usually**   **Seldom**   **Never**

b) I try to find out other people's suggestions for solving problems that puzzle me.

Always   **Usually**   **Seldom**   **Never**

c) I plan carefully to make sure I meet my deadlines.

Always   **Usually**   **Seldom**   **Never**

d) If someone is being difficult, I think carefully before making a response.

Always   **Usually**   **Seldom**   **Never**

e) I don't mind sharing my possessions or my time.

Always   **Usually**   **Seldom**   **Never**

f) I take account of other people's views and opinions.

Always   **Usually**   **Seldom**   **Never**

g) I enjoy thinking of new ways of doing things.

Always   **Usually**   **Seldom**   **Never**

h) I like creating new and different things.

Always   **Usually**   **Seldom**   **Never**

i) I enjoy planning and finding ways of solving problems.

Always   **Usually**   **Seldom**   **Never**

j) I enjoy getting feedback about my performance.

    Always   **Usually**   **Seldom**   **Never**

k) I try to learn from constructive criticism so that I know what to improve.

    Always   **Usually**   **Seldom**   **Never**

l) I enjoy new challenges.

    Always   **Usually**   **Seldom**   **Never**

m) I am even-tempered.

    Always   **Usually**   **Seldom**   **Never**

n) I am happy to make changes when necessary.

    Always   **Usually**   **Seldom**   **Never**

o) I like helping other people.

    Always   **Usually**   **Seldom**   **Never**

Score 3 points for each time you answered 'Always', 2 points for 'Usually', 1 point for 'Seldom' and 0 points for 'Never'. The higher your score, the higher your personal, learning and thinking skills.

2 How creative are you? Test yourself with this activity. Identify 50 different objects you could fit into a matchbox at the same time! As a start, three suitable items are a postage stamp, a grain of rice, a staple. Can you find 47 more?

BTEC FACTS

Your BTEC First qualification is at Level 2. Qualifications in functional skills start at Entry level and continue to Level 2. (You don't need to achieve functional skills to gain any BTEC qualification, and the evidence from a BTEC assignment can't be used towards the assessment of functional skills.)

Functional skills

Functional skills are the practical skills you need to function confidently, effectively and independently at work, when studying and in everyday life. They focus on the following areas:

- Information and Communications Technology (ICT)
- Maths
- English.

You may already be familiar with functional skills. Your BTEC First tutors will give you more information about how you will continue to develop these skills on your new course.

ICT skills

These will relate directly to how much 'hands-on' practice you have had on IT equipment. You may be an experienced IT user, and using word-processing, spreadsheet and presentation software may be second nature. Searching for information online may be something you do every day – in between downloading music, buying or selling on eBay and updating your Facebook profile!

Or you may prefer to avoid computer contact as much as possible. If so, there are two things you need to do.

1   Use every opportunity to improve your ICT skills so that you can start to live in the 21st century!

2   Make life easier by improving your basic proofreading and document preparation skills.

Proofreading and document preparation skills

Being able to produce well-displayed work quickly will make your life a lot easier. On any course there will be at least one unit that requires you to use good document preparation skills.

Tips to improve your document production skills

✔   If your keyboarding skills are poor, ask if there is a workshop you can join. Or your library or resource centre may have software you can use.

✔   Check that you know the format of documents you have to produce for assignments. It can help to have a 'model' version of each type in your folder for quick reference.

✔   Practise checking your work by reading word by word – and remember not to rely on spellcheckers (see page 60).

Activity: How good are your ICT skills?

1a)   Test your current ICT abilities by responding *honestly* to each of the following statements.

i)   I can create a copy of my timetable using a word-processing or spreadsheet package.
True   **False**

ii)   I can devise and design a budget for myself for the next three months using a spreadsheet package.
True   **False**

iii)   I can email a friend who has just got broadband to say how to minimise the danger of computer viruses, what a podcast is, and also explain the restrictions on music downloads.
True   **False**

iv)   I can use presentation software to prepare a presentation containing four or five slides on a topic of my choice.
True   **False**

v)   I can research online to compare the performance and prices of laptop computers and prepare an information sheet using word-processing software.
True   **False**

vi)   I can prepare a poster, with graphics, for my mother's friend, who is starting her own business preparing children's party food, and attach it to an email to her for approval.
True   **False**

TRY THIS

Learning to touch-type can save you hours of time. To check your keyboarding skills go to www. pearsonhotlinks.co.uk, insert the express code 5728S and click on the link for this page.

TOP TIPS

Print your work on good paper and keep it flat so that it looks good when you hand it in.

1b) Select any one of the above to which you answered false and learn how to do it.

2 Compare the two tables below. The first is an original document; the second is a typed copy. Are they identical? Highlight any differences you find and check them with the key on page 101.

Name	Date	Time	Room
Abbott	16 July	9.30 am	214
Grey	10 August	10.15 am	160
Johnston	12 August	2.20 pm	208
Waverley	18 July	3.15 pm	180
Jackson	30 September	11.15 am	209
Gregory	31 August	4.20 pm	320
Marshall	10 September	9.30 am	170
Bradley	16 September	2.20 pm	210

Name	Date	Time	Room
Abbott	26 July	9.30 am	214
Gray	10 August	10.15 am	160
Johnson	12 August	2.20 pm	208
Waverley	18 July	3.15 am	180
Jackson	31 September	11.15 am	209
Gregory	31 August	4.20 pm	320
Marshall	10 September	9.30 pm	170
Bradley	16 August	2.20 pm	201

Maths or numeracy skills

Four easy ways to improve your numeracy skills

1 Work out simple calculations in your head, like adding up the prices of items you are buying. Then check if you are correct when you pay for them.

2 Set yourself numeracy problems based on your everyday life. For example, if you are on a journey that takes 35 minutes and you leave home at 11.10am, what time will you arrive? If you are travelling at 40 miles an hour, how long will it take you to go 10 miles?

3 Treat yourself to a Maths Training program.

4 Check out online sites to improve your skills. Go to www.pearsonhotlinks.co.uk, insert the express code 5728S and click on the link for this page.

TOP TIPS

Quickly test answers. For example, if fuel costs 85p a litre and someone is buying 15 litres, estimate this at £1 x 15 (£15) and the answer should be just below this. So if your answer came out at £140, you'd immediately know you'd done something wrong!

Activity: How good are your maths skills?

Answer as many of the following questions as you can in 15 minutes. Check your answers with the key on page 101.

1 **a)** 12 + 28 = ?

   i) 30   ii) 34   iii) 38   iv) 40   v) 48

b) 49 ÷ 7 = ?

   i) 6   ii) 7   iii) 8   iv) 9   v) 10

c) ½ + 1¼ = ?

   i) ¾   ii) 1½   iii) 1¾   iv) 2¼   v) 3

d) 4 × 12 = 8 × ?

   i) 5   ii) 6   iii) 7   iv) 8   v) 9

e) 16.5 + 25.25 – ? = 13.25

   i) 28.5   ii) 31.25 iii) 34.5 iv) 41.65 v) 44

2 **a)** You buy four items at £1.99, two at 98p and three at £1.75. You hand over a £20 note. How much change will you get? _____

b) What fraction of one litre is 250 ml? _____

c) What percentage of £50 is £2.50? _____

d) A designer travelling on business can claim 38.2p a mile in expenses. How much is she owed if she travels 625 miles? _____

e) You are flying to New York in December. New York is five hours behind British time and the flight lasts eight hours. If you leave at 11.15 am, what time will you arrive? _____

f) For your trip to the United States you need American dollars. You find that the exchange rate is $1.5 dollars.

   i) How many dollars will you receive if you exchange £500? _____

   ii) Last year your friend visited New York when the exchange rate was $1.8. She also exchanged £500. Did she receive more dollars than you or fewer – and by how much? _____

g) A security guard and his dog patrol the perimeter fence of a warehouse each evening. The building is 480 metres long and 300 metres wide and the fence is 80 metres out from the building on all sides. If the guard and his dog patrol the fence three times a night, how far will they walk? _____

English skills

Your English skills affect your ability to understand what you read, prepare a written document, say what you mean and understand other people. Even if you're doing a practical subject, there will always be times when you need to leave someone a note, tell them about a phone call, read or listen to instructions – or write a letter for a job application!

Six easy ways to improve your English skills

1. Read more. It increases the number of words you know and helps to make you familiar with correct spellings.

2. Look up words you don't understand in a dictionary and check their meaning. Then try to use them yourself to increase your vocabulary.

3. Do crosswords. These help increase your vocabulary and practise your spelling at the same time.

4. You can use websites to help you get to grips with English vocabulary, grammar and punctuation. Go to www.pearsonhotlinks.co.uk, insert the express code 5728S and click on the link for this page.

5. Welcome opportunities to practise speaking in class, in discussion groups and during presentations – rather than avoiding them!

6. Test your ability to listen to someone else by seeing how much you can remember when they've finished speaking.

Activity: How good are your English skills?

1. In the table below are 'wrong' versions of words often spelled incorrectly. Write the correct spellings on the right. Check your list against the answers on page 101.

Incorrect spelling	Correct spelling
accomodation	
seperate	
definate	
payed	
desparate	
acceptible	
competant	
succesful	

2 Correct the error(s) in these sentences.

a) The plug on the computer is lose.

b) The car was stationery outside the house.

c) Their going on they're holidays tomorrow.

d) The principle of the college is John Smith.

e) We are all going accept Tom.

3 Punctuate these sentences correctly.

a) Toms train was late on Monday and Tuesday.

b) She is going to France Belgium Spain and Italy in the summer.

c) He comes from Leeds and says its great there.

4 Read the article on copyright.

Copyright

Anyone who uses a photocopier can break copyright law if they carry out unrestricted photocopying of certain documents. This is because The Copyright, Designs and Patents Act 1988 protects the creator of an original work against having it copied without permission.

Legally, every time anyone writes a book, composes a song, makes a film or creates any other type of artistic work, this work is treated as their property (or copyright). If anyone else wishes to make use of it, they must get permission to do so and, on occasions, pay a fee.

Licences can be obtained to allow educational establishments to photocopy limited numbers of some publications. In addition, copies of an original document can be made for certain specific purposes. These include research and private study. Under the Act, too, if an article is summarised and quoted by anyone, then the author and title of the original work must be acknowledged.

a) Test your ability to understand unfamiliar information by responding to the following statements with 'True' or 'False'.

i) Students and tutors in schools and colleges can copy anything they want.
True   False

ii) The law which covers copyright is The Copyright, Designs and Patents Act 1988.
True   False

iii) A student photocopying a document in the library must have a licence.
True   False

iv) Copyright only relates to books in the library.
True   False

v) If you quote a newspaper report in an assignment, you don't need to state the source.
True   False

vii) Anyone is allowed to photocopy a page of a book for research purposes.
True   False

b) Make a list of key points in the article, then write a brief summary in your own words.

5 Nikki has read a newspaper report that a horse racing in the Kentucky Derby had to be put down. The filly collapsed and the vet couldn't save her. Nikki says it's the third time in two years a racehorse has had to be put down in the US. As a horse lover she is convinced racing should be banned in Britain and the US. She argues that fox hunting was banned to protect foxes, and that racehorses are more important and more expensive than foxes. Darren disagrees. He says the law is not working, hardly anyone has been prosecuted and fox hunting is going on just like before. Debbie says that animals aren't important whilst there is famine in the world.

a) Do you think the three arguments are logical? See if you can spot the flaws and check your ideas with the suggestions on page 101.

b) Sporting activities and support for sporting teams often provoke strong opinions. For a sport or team of your choice, identify two opposing views that might be held. Then decide how you would give a balanced view. Test your ideas with a friend or family member.

Answers

Skills building answers

ICT activities

2 Differences between the two tables are highlighted in bold.

Name	Date	Time	Room
Abbott	**16** July	9.30 am	214
Grey	10 August	10.15 am	160
Johnston	12 August	2.20 pm	208
Waverley	18 July	3.15 **pm**	180
Jackson	**30** September	11.15 am	209
Gregory	31 August	4.20 pm	320
Marshall	10 September	9.30 **am**	170
Bradley	16 **September**	2.20 pm	**210**

Maths/numeracy activities

1 **a)** iv, **b)** ii, **c)** iii, **d)** ii, **e)** i

2 **a)** £4.83, **b)** ¼, **c)** 5%, **d)** £238.75, **e)** 2.15 pm, **f) i)** $750 **ii)** $150 dollars more, **g)** 6.6 km.

English activities

1 Spellings: accommodation, separate, definite, paid, desperate, acceptable, competent, successful

2 Errors:
a) The plug on the computer is <u>loose</u>.
b) The car was <u>stationary</u> outside the house.
c) <u>They're</u> going on <u>their</u> holidays tomorrow.
d) The <u>principal</u> of the college is John Smith.
e) We are all going <u>except</u> Tom.

3 Punctuation:
a) Tom's train was late on Monday and Tuesday.
b) She is going to France, Belgium, Spain and Italy in the summer.
c) He comes from Leeds and says it's great there.

4 **a) i)** False, **ii)** True, **iii)** False, **iv)** False, **v)** False, **vi)** False, **vii)** True

5 A logical argument would be that if racehorses are frequently injured in a particular race, eg one with difficult jumps, then it should not be held. It is not logical to compare racehorses with foxes. The value of the animal is irrelevant if you are assessing cruelty. Darren's argument is entirely different and unrelated to Nikki's. Whether or not fox hunting legislation is effective or not has no bearing on the danger (or otherwise) to racehorses. Finally, famine is a separate issue altogether. You cannot logically 'rank' problems in the world to find a top one and ignore the others until this is solved!

Accessing website links

Links to various websites are referred to throughout this BTEC Level 2 First Study Skills Guide. In order to ensure that these links are up to date, that they work and that the sites aren't inadvertently linked to any material that could be considered offensive, we have made the links available on our website: www.pearsonhotlinks.co.uk. When you visit the site, please enter the express code 5728S to gain access to the website links and information on how they can be used to help you with your studies.

Useful terms

Apprenticeships
Schemes that enable you to work and earn money at the same time as you gain further qualifications (an NVQ award and a technical certificate) and improve your functional skills. Apprentices learn work-based skills relevant to their job role and their chosen industry. Go to www.pearsonhotlinks.co.uk, insert the express code 5728S and click on the link for this useful term to find out more.

Assessment methods
Methods, such as practical tasks and assignments, which are used to check that your work demonstrates the learning and understanding you need to obtain the qualification.

Assessor
The tutor who marks or assesses your work.

Assignment
A complete task or mini-**project** set to meet specific grading criteria.

Assignment brief
The information and instructions related to a particular assignment.

BTEC Level 3 Nationals
Qualifications you can take when you have successfully achieved a Level 2 qualification, such as BTEC First. They are offered in a variety of subjects.

Credit value
The number of credits attached to your BTEC course. The credit value increases relative to the length of time you need to complete the course, from 15 credits for a BTEC Certificate, to 30 credits for a BTEC Extended Certificate and 60 credits for a BTEC Diploma.

Command word
The word in an assignment that tells you what you have to do to produce the type of answer that is required, eg 'list', 'describe', 'analyse'.

Educational Maintenance Award (EMA)
This is a means-tested award which provides eligible learners under 19 who are studying a full-time course at a centre with a cash sum of money every week. Go to www.pearsonhotlinks.co.uk, insert the express code 5728S and click on the link for this useful term to find out more.

Functional skills
The practical skills that enable all learners to use and apply English, Maths and ICT both at work and in their everyday lives. They aren't compulsory to achieve on the course, but are of great use to you.

Grade
The rating of pass, merit or distinction that is given to an assignment you have completed, which identifies the standard you have achieved.

Grading criteria
The standard you have to demonstrate to obtain a particular grade in the unit. In other words, what you have to prove you can do.

Grading grid
The table in each unit of your BTEC qualification specification that sets out the grading criteria.

Indicative reading
Recommended books, magazines, journals and websites whose content is both suitable and relevant to the unit.

Induction
A short programme of events at the start of a course or work placement designed to give you essential information and introduce you to other people so that you can settle in easily.

Internal verification
The quality checks carried out by nominated tutors at all centres to ensure that all assignments are at the right level and cover appropriate learning outcomes. The checks also ensure that all **assessors** are marking work consistently and to the same standards.

Learning outcomes

The learning and skills you must demonstrate to show that you have learned a unit effectively.

Levels of study

The depth, breadth and complexity of knowledge, understanding and skills required to achieve a qualification determines its level. Level 2 is equivalent to GCSE level (grades A* to C). Level 3 equates to GCE A-level. As you successfully achieve one level, you can progress on to the next. BTEC qualifications are offered at Entry Level, then Levels 1, 2, 3, 4, 5, 6 and 7.

Mandatory units

On a BTEC Level 2 First course, these are the compulsory units that all learners must complete to gain the qualification.

Optional units

Units on your course from which you may be able to make a choice. They help you specialise your skills, knowledge and understanding, and may help progression into work or further education.

Personal, learning and thinking skills (PLTS)

The skills and qualities that improve your ability to work independently and be more effective and confident at work. Opportunities for developing these are a feature of all BTEC First courses. They aren't compulsory to achieve on the course, but are of great use to you.

Plagiarism

Copying someone else's work or work from any other sources (eg the internet) and passing it off as your own. It is strictly forbidden on all courses.

Portfolio

A collection of work compiled by a learner – for an **assessor** – usually as evidence of learning.

Project

A comprehensive piece of work which normally involves original research and planning and investigation, either by an individual or a team. The outcome will vary depending upon the type of project undertaken. For example, it may result in the organisation of a specific event, a demonstration of a skill, a presentation, or a piece of writing.

Tutorial

An individual or small group meeting with your tutor at which you discuss the work you are currently doing and other more general course issues.

Unit content

Details about the topics covered by the unit and the knowledge and skills you need to complete it.

Work placement

Time spent on an employer's premises when you carry out work-based tasks as an employee and also learn about the enterprise to develop your skills and knowledge.

Work-related qualification

A qualification designed to help you to develop the knowledge and understanding you need for a particular area of work.